S0-BJB-591

OF LASTING INTEREST

By James Playsted Wood

OF LASTING INTEREST

THE STORY OF ADVERTISING

AN ELEPHANT IN THE FAMILY

THE BECKONING HILL

MAGAZINES IN THE UNITED STATES

Of Lasting Interest

The Story of The Reader's Digest

BY

JAMES PLAYSTED WOOD

DOUBLEDAY & COMPANY, INC.

Garden City, New York

1958

Library of Congress Catalog Card Number 58–13265

Printed in the United States of America
First Edition

for E . I . C .

PREFACE

New ideas in magazine communication are rare. There are not many such major ideas in a century. Daniel Defoe, who began publication of *The Review* in 1704, is generally credited with originating the idea of the magazine at all. Though he was imitating English originals, Benjamin Franklin had a new magazine idea when in 1741 he started *The General Magazine, and Historical Chronicle, for All the British Plantation in America. Godey's Lady's Book,* as a publication for women, was a new idea in 1830. Cyrus H. K. Curtis, with *Ladies' Home Journal* in 1883 and *The Saturday Evening Post,* when he began to publish it in 1897, developed the modern idea of using national advertising to support magazine publication. *Time,* as a weekly news magazine in 1923, and *Life,* as a photographic weekly in 1936, came as expressions of new magazine ideas. As a pocket-sized digest of articles selected and condensed from other periodicals, The Reader's Digest brought another new idea to magazine communication in 1922.

When it first appeared in February of that year, The Reader's Digest was a modest, pocket-sized, reprint magazine, an entirely new and different kind of periodical. Now, more than tripled in number of pages and published in many languages, it is the most widely read magazine in the world. Once purely a reflection of other periodicals, it has long since established an identity of its own, and the familiar Reader's Digest is itself reflected in contemporary life. About the only surviving example of personal journalism among mass magazines, it stands as a unique accomplishment in magazine editing and publishing.

For all of these and other reasons The Reader's Digest has long attracted scrutiny and appraisal. This book attempts a fairly close look at the information it disseminates, the entertainment it offers, and the attitudes it fosters. The effort has been to be accurate to the origins, the development, the production, and something of the significance of The Reader's Digest.

The book could not have been written without the full cooperation of DeWitt Wallace and Lila Acheson Wallace, who founded, edit, and publish The Reader's Digest, and that of the other editors and executives of the magazine. To all of them go my sincere thanks.

J.P.W.

CONTENTS

OF LASTING INTEREST

CHAPTER I

DEWITT WALLACE AND HIS FIRST PUBLISHING VENTURES

The Reader's Digest is the largest, the most widely read, and possibly the most influential magazine in the world.

Since February 1922, when its first issue appeared, it has been an incontrovertible fact of American life. Since 1938, when the first of its foreign editions was established, it has been an American fact of international life. "The Little Magazine," as it proudly described itself when it was considered by its editors and readers alike as a service to a few thousand subscribers, has been called, and perhaps is, "the greatest common denominator in communications we have."

The Digest's accomplishment is almost incredible. By all the laws and bylaws of business and the harsh ground rules of the highly competitive magazine-publishing industry in the United States, it should have been impossible. The amazing success of The Reader's Digest has called forth inarticulate exclamation, dismay, extravagant admiration, envy, bitter derision, and unsuccessful imitation. It has given rise to rumor, fiction, sometimes deliberate misrepresentation—none of it any more incredible than the simple facts.

By certified count of the independent Audit Bureau of Circulations, The Reader's Digest has a monthly circulation in the United States of well over 12,000,000, almost twice the circulation of the next largest American magazine. The Reader's Digest is read every month by a survey-measured 32,000,000 Americans, reaching one in every four adults in the nation.

Published now in 30 editions in 13 different languages for reading in countries all over the globe, The Reader's Digest has a world circulation of almost 21,000,000 copies for reading every month by an estimated 70,000,000 men and women. Somehow the Digest has learned to talk to a significant part of the world's population in language that is universally understood about things which seemingly people everywhere value and believe.

At The Reader's Digest editorial offices on its 80-acre estate of park and wooded hills outside of Chappaqua, New York, some forty miles north of New York City, nearly 100 editors and sub-editors read, cut, reread, and rework the rich and widely varied material that goes into each issue.

Nearly 2500 clerical workers, hundreds more during peak seasons, work on the Digest's vast subscription and circulation operations. The Digest's art, advertising, and promotion departments hum with activity on Park Avenue in New York. There are Reader's Digest offices and editors in New York, London, Paris, Copenhagen, Havana, Helsinki, Quebec, Madrid, Milan, Oslo, Rio de Janiero, Stockholm, Stuttgart, Sydney, Toronto, and Tokyo. Other Digest editors and writers travel the world continually in search of material for the magazine.

In Dayton, Ohio, the high-speed, Goss five-color presses of the McCall Corporation spin out a half million Reader's Digests a day, using 50,000 tons of paper a year. Presses in the countries for which they are published devour another 34,000 tons of paper annually to turn out additional millions of Digests every month in French, German, Spanish, Portuguese, Japanese, Danish, Norwegian, Swedish, Dutch, Italian, Finnish, and Arabic. The United States, Swedish, Japanese, German, and Spanish editions are published also in Braille, and the domestic edition is recorded on talking records for the blind. There is a tape recording for the blind in Germany.

The Reader's Digest Condensed Book Club, founded in 1950, is by far the largest book club in the world, with more members than the two next largest book clubs combined. Quarterly it publishes in volumes of about 575 pages each condensations of popular current books. Nearly 12 million Reader's Digest Condensed Books are printed every year on a new offset press in the huge Sharon Hill plant of The Curtis Publishing Company a few miles south of Philadelphia. The roaring "Green Hornet," as the mighty five-color Levey press has been dubbed by its crew, consumes 1200 feet of paper a minute, printing 144 Condensed Book pages at a time in three signatures of 48 pages each.

The spread and penetration of The Reader's Digest in the United States and around the world have never been approximated by any other periodical. It is unlikely they will soon be surpassed. The Reader's Digest on many counts is easily the phenomenon of twentieth-century mass magazines.

The Reader's Digest is read far and wide by high and low. It is read by those who read widely and intensively and by those who read little else. It is read from the pulpit and the judicial bench, read on trains and aboard ships and planes, studied in the schoolroom, read and reread in the home. Nationwide studies conducted by random sampling methods in 1957 found that an average issue of The Reader's Digest is picked up for reading 168,000,000 times a month.

People read the Digest with willing belief and quote it as authority. They look forward pleasurably to the arrival of their monthly issues and greet them with the affection they feel for a friend. They prize the Digest for the variety of its contents, for its warmth and humanness, its factual accuracy, its common sense, its humor. They believe that the Digest gives them the best of all that appears in the other magazines; they know it gives them a lift of the spirit. They look to the Digest for news and explanation of what is new and for the comfort of what is old and sustaining. When the Digest speaks out bluntly in controversy, and it does, it carries conviction of its own forthrightness and strengthens their own beliefs. Again and again The Reader's Digest has demonstrated its force in the affairs of men, but, more often and more strongly, in the day-to-day lives of men and women as individuals.

It is the Digest's universality of appeal, the faith and trust it evokes in its readers on every continent, that makes the story of The Reader's Digest and of the ideas and people behind it one of absorbing and compelling interest.

The story began, as it remains, with DeWitt Wallace.

DeWitt Wallace was born in St. Paul, Minnesota, November 12, 1889, the fifth child of Dr. James Wallace, who was first professor, then dean, then president of struggling, Presbyterian-related Macalester College. The boy's mother was Janet Davis Wallace, daughter of the Rev. T. K. Davis, the librarian of the College of Wooster in Ohio. James Wallace, who was also a Presbyterian preacher, though not an ordained minister, had come to Macalester College from the Wooster faculty as professor of Greek and Modern Languages.

Dr. Wallace wrote the child's maternal grandmother a few days after Thanksgiving, 1889: "Janet thinks it is a very superior baby, while I am noncommittal on the subject. It is too soon to formulate an opinion . . . Janet wants to call him James, but I object . . . So I guess we will call him Anonymous for a while." The name DeWitt, later given the child, was that of an uncle of Dr. Wallace.

A little later Dr. Wallace had definitely formulated opinions about his young son. He wrote his wife while she was visiting at her home in Wooster: "The baby is a rogue, a rascal, a bandit, a thief, a vandal, without character or reputation—utterly lawless, wandering where he will and in all kinds of mischief."

Macalester was in continual financial straits. Faculty salaries, generally in arrears, were sometimes not paid at all. Dr. Wallace, imbued with the belief that there should be a Presbyterian college in Minnesota, persisted and endured, and his family with him. As a daughter put it years later, there was "too much cold house and irregular salary."

To save expenses while her husband traveled, canvassing to raise funds for Macalester, Janet Wallace often returned to Wooster with her young children for long periods. Thus, DeWitt Wallace grew up in Ohio as well as in frontier Minnesota. The Wallace children were unconscious of hardship or privation, though once, at any rate, so a biographer of Dr. James Wallace records, DeWitt Wallace announced with some vehemence, "I want to live in a house that my papa owns and *nobody else* so I can dig a hole in the yard."

As a child he narrowly escaped precocity. His marks in the

early grades were so high that he was pushed rapidly ahead, skipping two school years. One result was that DeWitt Wallace entered Macalester Academy much younger than his classmates. He was, uncomfortably, the only boy still in knickerbockers. Wallace rescued himself from this embarrassment through the discovery that there were other and more satisfactory things in life than books and family prayers. Games fascinated, and he threw himself into every sport he could find. To his family's displeasure but his own content, his grades plummeted after his second year in the academy. They stayed marginal for the rest of his haphazard academic career.

Wallace first escaped Macalester when his father consented to let him attend the Mt. Hermon School for boys, which the evangelist Dwight L. Moody had founded in Northfield, Massachusetts. This environment also proved constricting. For participating too zealously in a dormitory rumpus near the end of the second semester, DeWitt Wallace and several companions were ordered to move to another dormitory. Instead of complying, he and a fellow conspirator slipped out and made their way to Boston. After seeing the sights of Boston for a week, they went on to New York. In New York, California looked even more attractive. For fifty dollars each they were able to buy train tickets to San Francisco. Here—and the accomplishment still rather pleases DeWitt Wallace—they progressed triumphantly through a series of construction jobs, each at a higher rate of pay, without losing a day's work.

Having seen this much of the world, DeWitt Wallace entered Macalester College in the fall of 1907. Soon he was specializing in football, hockey, and baseball, excelling at second base. Restless, curious, but more interested in the world about him than in the past, he did not allow assigned studies to interfere appreciably with his pleasures. Scholastically he fell far short of the standards set for the son of President James Wallace, M.A., Ph.D., D.D., LL.D.

DeWitt Wallace was far happier working summers in the Montana hayfields or playing semipro baseball in Leeds, North Dakota. At the end of his sophomore year at Macalester he took off for a summer job in the bank of an uncle, Robert Wallace, in Monte Vista, Colorado. Colorado was a freer place than the Macalester campus in St. Paul. DeWitt Wallace liked it so well that, instead of remaining only for the summer, he stayed in Monte Vista and his bank job for a full year.

It was an important year for DeWitt Wallace.

He was reading widely in current publications. Often alone in his room at night with little to do, he began work at a task which appealed to him. Some of the magazine articles he was reading seemed to be of more than passing interest and value. Wallace began keeping a card file of the high points of what seemed to him the best articles. The pastime became an absorbing interest. During the fall and winter of 1909–10, even before he recognized the idea, DeWitt Wallace began practicing the technique that, after several mutations and tribulations enough, was to lead to The Reader's Digest twelve years later.

When the opening of the college year rolled around again, DeWitt Wallace decided against return to the confines of Macalester. He wanted broader fields, and he liked California. He returned to San Francisco and enrolled in the College of Social Sciences of the University of California in Berkeley. Tall, lean, handsome, hardened by sports and work outdoors, Wallace found the university more to his liking than Presbyterian and provincial

Macalester. There were more people and more different kinds of people. Psi Upsilon provided a different kind of social life than he had known at the little college in St. Paul. Studies were even less bothersome. Wallace concentrated his efforts during two more undergraduate years—by his own smiling but rather rueful confession—on being "The Playboy of the Western World."

It was pleasant, but by the end of his second year in Berkeley Wallace had had enough of academe.

He went home to St. Paul and a job writing sales-promotion letters in the Book Department of the Webb Publishing Company, which at that time issued *The Farmer, The Farmer's Wife,* and a series of high-school textbooks. During the four years he spent with Webb, Wallace noted the excellence and variety of the pamphlets on scores of subjects issued by the United States Department of Agriculture and the state agricultural experiment stations. His imagination was stimulated, and an idea took form—rather, it was the development of the idea which had been quietly germinating beneath his restlessness ever since his first attempts at digesting magazine articles in Monte Vista.

Many of these free agricultural publications, he thought, would be very useful to farmers, most of whom did not know they existed. There was no one place where the farmer could obtain information about what published materials were available on any specific subject. DeWitt Wallace began to list titles, then groups of titles, together with brief descriptions of the content of each publication. His work began to take form.

Wallace left his job, obtained credit from the Webbs, and had his listings set up and printed on good stock in a booklet of 120 pages titled *Getting the Most Out of Farming.* The cover described it as "A Selected List of Publications of Value by the Government and State Experiment Stations." It was "Prepared by DeWitt Wallace" and issued, 1916, from the press of the Webb Publishing Company, St. Paul.

The contents of what was the first published forerunner of The Reader's Digest were classified by subject: Agricultural Clubs, Alfalfa, Apples, Bees, Broom Corn, Children, Diseases of Animals, Diseases of Plants, Education. . . . Proverbs and bits of penny wisdom were printed in boxes along with the running heads at the tops of the pages:

Know that your seed will grow. Test—don't guess.

If the bulletins on peaches—and other subjects—were published by private companies, you would pay dearly for them.

Build right the first time—alterations are expensive.

If you can't go to college—let the college come to you.

Wallace sold his service not direct to farmers but to banks for free distribution to their farmer customers, space being left on the cover of the booklet for the bank to imprint its name. The booklets went well, so well in Minnesota that Wallace bought an old Model T Ford touring car and started west. He bumped along from town to town, canvassing the banks as he went, often sleeping in the flivver with his sample copies of *Getting the Most Out of Farming* at night. He toured North Dakota, Montana, and parts of Oregon and Washington. Finally he sold 100,000 copies of the booklet before he returned to St. Paul.

Encouraged by this success, Wallace, who had at least cleared expenses, sought further application of his idea. He began to digest ideas from advertising and merchandising trade journals and to sell this service designed especially for department stores in country towns. The department-store venture was soon abandoned.

Pondering these two experiences as he lay awake one summer night in a hayfield bunkhouse in Montana, DeWitt Wallace had a sudden realization. He had thought first in terms of agricultural, then of business digests. These were specific and specialized applications. The digest idea could as easily be applied to the general—to the condensation of articles of lasting interest from the leading magazines for reading by a wider public.

This new idea simmering in his mind, Wallace returned once more to St. Paul, where he took a bread-and-butter job as manager of the Mail Order Department of Brown & Bigelow, manufacturers of calendars and greeting cards. He was not to remain there long, for this was 1916.

When in April 1917 the United States declared war on Germany, DeWitt Wallace, who immediately volunteered, became one of the first twenty-five men to leave St. Paul for service. This impatient patriotism he ascribes entirely to his enthusiasm for escaping the insupportable dullness of his job.

A sergeant-instructor at Fort Dodge, Iowa, he volunteered again, this time for demotion to private and immediate duty overseas. He was again a sergeant and in France with the 35th Infantry Division by April 1918. By the fifth day of the Meuse-Argonne offensive, October 1, 1918, half his company had been killed or wounded. The survivors were about to be withdrawn when DeWitt Wallace caught part of a shrapnel burst in the neck and abdomen. A fragment pierced his nose, and a splinter lodged in his lung.

The neck wound was the most serious. The first doctor to

reach him after he had been evacuated behind the lines exclaimed that the shrapnel had just missed the larynx.

"Then what?" asked Wallace, though he could hardly speak.

"You would never have talked again."

The second examining medic affably observed that the shrapnel had come close to severing Wallace's jugular vein. "The only way we could stop the bleeding then would be by choking you to death."

A third doctor was more concerned about the flesh wound over Wallace's abdomen. "One of the worst places you could be hit."

Wallace spent four months recovering at the army general hospital at Aix-les-Bains. His long convalescence gave him the first opportunity he had had to work uninterrupted at the idea which had become almost an obsession since its first glimmerings in Colorado in 1909 and 1910. The hospital was plentifully supplied with American magazines. Wallace read all he could lay his hands on. Here was rich material. If the best were selected, it could be made available in one publication to people who could not possibly read all the important magazines. There was another point. Most of the pieces, it seemed to him, were far too long. A reader was forced to wade through an author's prolixity to reach firm ground at all. Many of the articles, he believed, could be cut by three-quarters and still retain their essential meaning. Wallace got paper and pencil and went to work.

CHAPTER II

THE SAMPLE READER'S DIGEST OF 1920; LILA BELL ACHESON

DeWitt Wallace was discharged from the army in April 1919 at point of debarkation, Norfolk, Virginia. Unlike many men returning from combat in any large-scale war, he knew exactly what he wanted to do. In the A.E.F. hospital at Aix-les-Bains he had found that he could satisfactorily condense articles of what he considered lasting interest from the current magazines, and he was convinced that condensed articles of varied appeal could be collected and successfully published in a small monthly magazine.

Back in St. Paul once more, he made no attempt to find a job. He was too impatient to be at work on the idea which fascinated him, and tingling with envisioned possibilities. An aunt was a librarian in the Minneapolis Public Library, a circumstance which made shelf material more readily available.

Every day and all day for six months Wallace worked intently in the library, testing, experimenting, practicing. He searched through not only the current issues of the magazines, but also issues that were one to ten years old, for the kind of articles he wanted, then condensed them to bring out their salient points in brief, readable versions. Some, he found, he could cut by as much as 75 per cent, yet still retain their substance and the author's style and approach. Most of the articles, he believed, were improved when fat and filler were sliced away, sinews knit, muscles tensed. Meanings were made clear and they could be more quickly grasped. He developed a sharp eye and a practiced skill.

Early in 1920, satisfied that he had developed his idea to the point where he could present it fully formed, Wallace carefully selected a group of his digests, gave the collection the title he had been using in his own mind, and had several hundred copies of a sample magazine printed.

This first trial issue of DeWitt Wallace's original magazine is as recognizable today as any recent issue of The Reader's Digest. All the essential ingredients of The Reader's Digest were in it. Magazine title, brief articles selected and condensed from many sources, pocket size, even the price as it was to remain for many years—even the blurbs for articles in issues to come—were all there. This dummy magazine, which was not a dummy at all but a full-fledged unique periodical, was:

THE
READER'S
DIGEST

31 ARTICLES EACH MONTH FROM LEADING MAGAZINES,
EACH ARTICLE OF ENDURING VALUE AND INTEREST,
IN CONDENSED AND PERMANENT FORM
JANUARY, 1920
Published monthly by The Reader's Digest Association
Globe Bldg., St. Paul, Minnesota. DeWitt Wallace, Editor
25 cents a copy; $3.00 a year

The thirty-one articles had been selected from the *Literary Digest*, *Woman's Home Companion*, the *American Magazine*, *The New Republic*, *Country Life*, *Vanity Fair*, *National Geographic*, *Ladies' Home Journal*, *Atlantic Monthly*, *Outlook*, *Scribner's*, *Theatre Magazine*, *The Saturday Evening Post*, *McClure's*, and other magazines of the day. The articles included, "Is Honesty the Best Policy?", "Men vs. Women as an Audience," "The Shortest Route to the Top," "The Art of Opening a Conversation," "How to Regulate Your Weight," "What People Laugh At," "How We Get Our Styles," "Taking the Water Out of the Cost of Living," "America's Most Popular Crime." Humor, sex, health, day-to-day human interests, art of living material applicable to the life of the average person, what have become key Digest subjects were all represented. There were humorous departments, "The Spice of Life" and "Remarkable Remarks."

Filler spots at the end of articles were used for Digest promotion: "To acquire knowledge is not easy—few of us have the time. You can acquire a broad understanding of the world—a liberal education—in a pleasurable way by reading The Reader's Digest"; "If you enjoy—and you will—'The Art of Opening a Conversation' (page 57) you will also like 'To Bore or Not to Bore,' and 'How We Talk,' to appear in the February issue."

The title page of what was headed Vol. 1, No. 1 of The Reader's Digest carried a list of the qualities in his project which DeWitt Wallace hoped would convince publishers that here was a periodical worthy of adoption. They were written and presented as if to possible subscribers or newsstand purchasers. The Reader's Digest was a service to busy readers. It enabled the reader to learn something really worth while every day. "Because of its 'boiled down' interest and pocket size—the most practical and pleasant means of utilizing odd moments." The Digest was "the one magazine containing articles only of such *permanent* and *popular interest* that each issue will be of as great value a year or two hence as on the date of publication." It was "The Magazine of 100% Educational *Interest* . . . no articles on purely transient topics and no articles of limited or specialized appeal."

Wallace was elated. This was not only the culmination of his months of intensive effort and planning, it was also a dream made reality. He knew his article material had variety, color, and interest. He had worked and reworked his sales appeals. He had set the pattern for The Reader's Digest as to editorial content and format and as a publishing venture. He was sure of his editorial judgments, certain of the value of what he had produced, but moody, pessimistic, alternately fearful and hopeful of the results. He sent copies off quickly to the leading magazine publishers, offering The Reader's Digest for periodical publication. He talked with publishers he knew in the St. Paul-Minneapolis area. He showed copies to his friends.

His friends were polite but unimpressed. The publishers could not have cared less.

Rejections came one after another from every quarter. They were flat and final even from editors and publishers who knew him and had been familiar with his project as he worked on it. Horace Klein, one of the partners of the Webb Publishing Company, returned from a trip to New York with convincing proof that the whole idea was ridiculous. Fiction predominated in the popular magazines. Gertrude Battles Lane, well-known editor of *Woman's Home Companion,* had told Klein that the magazines carried articles only as window dressing for the advertisers. Of the other publishers who bothered to respond at all only William

Randolph Hearst was at all encouraging. He thought The Reader's Digest might in time reach a peak circulation of perhaps 300,000. It was too small a venture for him to undertake.

DeWitt Wallace, who had gambled everything on the attempt, was bitterly discouraged. He was still convinced that what he had done and was trying to do was good, but the evidence that The Reader's Digest was not acceptable to publishers was clear and complete. Understandably he could not then view this rejection of the Digest for what he later realized it was—an initial stroke of good fortune. He would have given The Reader's Digest to any publisher who would retain him as its editor.

In the midst of his depression Wallace found a convert and ally.

While an undergraduate in California, DeWitt Wallace had spent a Christmas vacation in Tacoma, Washington, at the home of Barclay Acheson, a Macalester college mate whose father also was a Presbyterian minister. In Tacoma he had met and been attracted to Acheson's sister, Lila, who had already announced her engagement. In January 1920 Wallace met Acheson, by now a Presbyterian minister with a relief organization, who told him that his sister was now neither married nor engaged. Lila, who had attended fashionable Ward-Belmont in Nashville, then graduated from the University of Oregon, was doing social work among workingwomen in New York.

Though he had not seen slight, blue-eyed, delicately featured Lila Bell Acheson in eight years, DeWitt Wallace immediately dispatched a ten-word telegram:

CONDITIONS AMONG WOMEN WORKERS IN SAINT PAUL GHASTLY URGE IMMEDIATE INVESTIGATION.

A week later—coincidence, not collusion—Lila Bell Acheson was sent to Minneapolis to establish an industrial Y.W.C.A.

Where DeWitt Wallace was still struggling toward a start, Canadian-born Lila Bell Acheson was already active and successful in a busy career. A young English teacher in the State of Washington, she had been recruited for war work at the outbreak of World War I when, for the first time in history, American women were flocking into industry. After training in New York under a program jointly sponsored by the U. S. Department of Labor and the Y.W.C.A., she was placed in charge of thirty social workers, most of them older than she, at the Industrial Service Center of a large Du Pont munitions plant in Pompton Lakes, New Jersey.

High employee turnover, a frightening accident rate, both sleepiness and insomnia were the immediate problems. Social acceptance of the women workers was another. Operating under wartime pressure, the great plant worked around the clock. Lila Bell Acheson and her staff worked around the clock with it to ameliorate working conditions and destroy some of the hindrances to production.

The company built a new social center to supplant outgrown quarters over the Y.W.C.A. Recreational work here combined with classes and social events of many kinds was the first step. Plant accidents were most frequent on the night shift. At the midnight lunch hour the girls would leave their benches and machines, eat a cold sandwich, and go to sleep on the floor around the heating pipes. Then they went groggily back to work and a multiplicity of mishaps, many of them serious. Hot lunches, all the hot coffee the girls could drink, music, and dancing were introduced at the midnight break. Employee turnover was markedly reduced, and the accident ratio declined until accidents were almost nil.

Overtired nightworkers could not sleep. Tense and restless, they wandered about the town. Lila Bell Acheson had them brought to the shore of Pompton Lake in company trucks. Coffee was waiting. Bacon sizzled over open fires. Recreational workers staged games and entertainment. The women workers ate, drank, relaxed, went home, and slept.

Residents of the area resented the crowds of girls in baggy factory garb on their streets. Meetings were held with various organizations reminding their members that these girls made the munitions that the United States and her allies were using against the enemy. The atmosphere changed. Townspeople began to help at the center, cooking, teaching, assisting with a Christmas pageant. Lila Bell Acheson pressed town toughs into service as proud hosts. The toughest girls from the plant proudly poured tea before the bright open fire in the clubroom.

"Nothing too difficult," Lila Acheson Wallace remembers, "but fun to correct." Her instinctive skill with people helped get things done. It was immoral, Barclay Acheson used to complain, for anyone to know as much about a person as his sister knew on first meeting someone.

After the armistice, Lila Acheson was sent by the same organization to do work of the same kind in other industrial centers. In New Orleans she found a beautiful old home on Magazine Street, had it refurbished, convinced the cotton-mill and tobacco-factory owners of the need for a decent social life for their women workers, and made it a social center for the girls, many of whom came from tragic homes. In time the center had a small restaurant, living rooms where the girls could entertain their friends, a dance floor, and eventually classes in music, languages, homemaking, some of the arts—and, most appreciated on hot summer nights in New Orleans, shower baths.

Success on these assignments led to Lila Bell Acheson's appointment as head of a new social-service department started by the Presbyterian Board of Home Missions. Young and charmingly persuasive, she spent much of her time in speaking and fund-raising, convincing audiences on the West Coast waterfront, on the Mesabi Iron Range in northern Minnesota, and in the Labor Temple in New York. She was traveling the country from Boston to San Francisco and back when she was borrowed by the Inter-Church World Movement for work among the migrant families who harvest crops from Biloxi, Mississippi, north into New England and New York State.

Again persuasion was the first step. Lila Bell Acheson had to convince the canners of the value of the program. They built the centers, schools, and nurseries she asked. College girls were recruited to work during their summer vacations in the migrant camps. Women residents of the small canning towns were made to see that their towns needed the workers as much as the workers needed the jobs. "When they saw the mothers who had been working hard in the canneries rushing to the nursery at their noon hour, hugging their babies who were bathed and fed and dressed beyond anything they could have dreamed of, no further urging was necessary."

Fully alive, warm with a sense of accomplishment, the young woman who came to Minneapolis already had three jobs and was being lent from one to the other. Before she left Minneapolis, she had accepted both DeWitt Wallace and the digest-periodical idea which every publisher had rejected. From that point, The

Reader's Digest has been a joint venture of DeWitt Wallace and Lila Bell Acheson.

Soon after Lila Acheson returned to New York, DeWitt Wallace, fired with a new interest in life, found a job in the newly organized International Publicity Department of the Westinghouse Electric and Manufacturing Company in Pittsburgh. He was the last man hired for the new department. He was the first man fired when, six months later, Westinghouse was struck by the depression of 1921. His department head explained that it was not only Wallace's junior status, but also the fact that it was known he wanted to start a new magazine, which led to the decision to discharge him.

At Westinghouse, Wallace had shown one of the sample copies of The Reader's Digest to a fellow worker. The other, who had had mail-order experience, read it from cover to cover that evening and was enthusiastic about its possibilities. He felt strongly that it could be sold successfully by mail and urged Wallace to try it. The day he was fired Wallace returned to his room and determinedly sat down and wrote his first circular appealing for subscribers to the projected periodical.

For three months he remained in Pittsburgh mailing circular letters, each with an individually typed opening page. He sent the circulars to lists of teachers and nurses. He collected a trunk full of college catalogues and sent his appeals for provisional subscriptions to the names of faculty members. He called on women's clubs and women's professional groups, soliciting subscriptions for the still nonexistent Reader's Digest.

The die was cast. Had he not been fired from Westinghouse, Wallace might never have had the courage to start the venture on his own. Now he was under way on his own. His appeals were bringing in responses and remittances with them. Wallace raced to New York and continued to write and mail his circulars.

On October 15, 1921, Barclay Acheson officiating, Wallace and Lila Bell Acheson were married in a church in Pleasantville in northern Westchester County. Mrs. Wallace had found a garden apartment at Macdougal and Bleecker streets in the Greenwich Village section of New York. They rented a basement room under a Village speak-easy of the Prohibition era at 1 Minetta Lane for office and storeroom. Before they went off to the Poconos on their wedding trip they mailed the last circular appeal Wallace had written. When they returned bundles of letters awaited them. Remittances enclosed, added to those from the Pittsburgh mailings, brought the total to nearly $5000. They borrowed another $1300 and placed an order with a Pittsburgh printer for 5000 copies of the first issue of The Reader's Digest.

Volume 1, Number 1 of The Reader's Digest appeared February 1922 with DeWitt Wallace and Lila Bell Acheson as co-founders, co-editors, and co-owners.

CHAPTER III

THE FIRST READER'S DIGEST, FEBRUARY 1922

When the copies of the first issue of The Reader's Digest were received at 1 Minetta Lane—euphonious Greenwich Village address which delighted both DeWitt Wallace and Lila Acheson Wallace—the editors hired habitués of the speak-easy upstairs and girls from a community club down the street to help wrap and address them to the trusting 1500 who, sight unseen, had risked charter subscriptions. Bundling the mail sacks into a cab, they rushed them to the post office. Then, dirty, tired, elated, DeWitt Wallace almost unbelieving, they drank a toast to the new magazine's success.

That rare first issue of The Reader's Digest was simple and unpretentious in appearance. There were no illustrations. There was no color. There was no fiction. There were no advertisements. There were 62 pages exclusive of the covers, which were of the same white paper stock as the inside pages. The title was accurate—the new magazine was a digest, and it was designed for the reader. Important part of DeWitt Wallace's basic discovery was that magazine articles could be written to please the reader, to give him the nub of the matter in the new, fast-moving world of the 1920s, instead of being written at length and with literary embellishments to please the author or the editor.

Under The Reader's Digest logotype which appeared in public for the first time was a small circular line drawing of an idealized woman, done after the Beardsley manner, writing with a huge quill on a partially unrolled scroll. It was an ornament the Pittsburgh printer happened to have in his case. There had been no money to spare for art. Under the ornament was the legend only slightly changed from the statement of 1920:

THIRTY-ONE ARTICLES EACH MONTH FROM LEADING MAGAZINES
—EACH ARTICLE OF ENDURING VALUE AND INTEREST
IN CONDENSED AND COMPACT FORM

The contents were listed on the inside of the front cover. Facing it on the first editorial page was "A Word of Thanks," signed by Lila Bell Acheson, for Mrs. Wallace retained her maiden name on the masthead of the Digest until March 1938. The editorial stressed the four features which it was believed that charter subscribers "will find of even greater value and interest than you had anticipated." These features were the 31 articles—one a day—condensed from leading periodicals, their enduring value and interest, the compact form of the magazine, and the means The Reader's Digest provided of "keeping one's information account open."

Essential characteristics and attitudes of The Reader's Digest were apparent in this initial issue.

The opening article, condensed from extracts in the *American Magazine,* was "How to Keep Young Mentally." In "Remarkable Remarks," from *The Independent and the Weekly Review,* Billy Sunday's choir leader, Homer Rodeheaver, was quoted:

"One cigarette will kill a cat." Billy Sunday himself said: "Try praising your wife, even if it does frighten her at first."

From the *Delineator* there was "Love—Luxury or Necessity?" from the *Outlook* there was "Wanted—Motives for Motherhood," from a book by Albert Payson Terhune was "Watch Your Dog and Be Wise." There were inspirational bits about heroes, Edison, Ford, and Stefansson; and there was a forthright exposé of brutality and sadism in "Prison Facts," condensed from the *Atlantic Monthly*.

Six of the articles in this first published issue of The Reader's Digest were pieces DeWitt Wallace had selected, condensed, tried, and tested in his sample Digest two years before. These were the page of "Remarkable Remarks"; "Whatever Is New for Women Is Wrong" from *Ladies' Home Journal;* "The Firefly's Light" from *Country Life;* "Useful Points in Judging People" from a book titled *Art and Science of Selling;* "Is the Stage Too Vulgar?" from *Theatre Magazine;* and "Progress in Science" from *Scientific American* and *Popular Science Monthly*. Each of these represented what were to become characteristic Reader's Digest interests—women, nature, art of living, morals, science, and a book excerpt.

One of these articles provided the inevitable typographical error which authenticates the first edition. Its title as listed in the table of contents posed an even neater question than was intended. It appeared as "Is the State Too Vulgar?"

The first Reader's Digest contained no advertising. The Digest was to publish strong attacks on advertising abuses. It was not to carry advertising itself for another 33 years, but this first issue contained "Advertising and Public Health," an article by Royal S. Copeland, then New York City's Health Commissioner, condensed from *Printers' Ink.* A box in bold-face type at the opening of the article read: "Advertising has changed the way we dress, the things we eat, our beds, our ideas of ventilation, our routine of living, the very fixtures in our bathrooms. Advertising has contributed materially to the lengthening of human life." A similar box, a digest of each digest, preceded every article in all the early issues of The Reader's Digest.

Humor, inspiration, sex, science, youth, self-improvement—DeWitt Wallace had selected the contents of this all-important first issue of The Reader's Digest with agonizing care, and he had covered the periodical field. Besides those already mentioned, there were condensed articles from the *Century, Woman's Home Companion, Scribner's, Review of Reviews, Mentor, House Beautiful, Asia, Current History, World's Work, Physical Culture, Good Housekeeping, Nation's Business, Hearst's International, Judge, Living Age,* and *McClure's.*

He had chosen widely from the popular, the literary, the cultural, the shelter, the humorous, and the women's magazines. He had included bits from the popular columnists of the time, Heywood Broun and Arthur Brisbane; used "Advice from a President's Physician," by Rear Admiral Cary T. Grayson, as the Digest's first health article; and even tapped commercial wisdom from a textbook issued by the National Salesman's Training Association.

Included wherever there was space were advertisements and promotional bits for The Reader's Digest itself. "'When a man stops learning he stops living.' Knowledge means power; the well-informed man is the strong man. Consider the information value of The Reader's Digest in the course of a year." One of the briefest of the condensations presented Theodore Roosevelt,

Thomas Edison, Abraham Lincoln, Lloyd George, and Lord Northcliffe as men who read, studied, looked about them, and asked questions in an eternal search for facts. Blurbs for articles that would appear in the March issue were scattered through the pages. "'The Woman Who Should Marry' will appear in the next issue, a 'most exquisitely daring summing up of the aims and destinies of women. Every woman will be interested in this article for in it she will find either her justification or her condemnation.'" Some of these teaser lines were from the test issue of 1920, more of whose articles would appear in later Digests.

There was even a portent of the later international interests of The Reader's Digest in one boxed blurb.

The Japanese film censor heartlessly nips all kissing scenes, pastes them together, and accumulates some thousands of feet of film kisses of every style and period for private view only.

The study of flower arrangement extends over five years of the Japanese girl's life.

The master of the Japanese house must have his beauty sleep.

In Japan one hears this wish: "May all pain be absent from important parts."

These and other fascinating insights into Japanese life will appear in an article in The Reader's Digest for March.

The inside of the back cover of Volume 1, Number 1 of The Reader's Digest reminded charter subscribers that the Digest had come into being because they felt—even before they could see a copy—that such a magazine would fill a need. The note emphasized what was to remain one of the Digest's strongest appeals for the next seven years, "The Reader's Digest is to be regarded as an exclusive *service* to members of our Association." Readers were urged to bring the new magazine to the attention of their friends. A subscription order blank was printed below the message.

The sales pressure was desperately necessary. Much of the Wallaces' capital had been expended in production of the first issue of The Reader's Digest. At the moment of mingled triumph and exhaustion that first publication day DeWitt Wallace knew with fearful certainty that unless the first issue succeeded and new subscriptions brought in more money there might be a second, but never a third or a fourth.

CHAPTER IV

THE MOVE TO PLEASANTVILLE

With the first issue of The Reader's Digest in the mails but its reception still uncertain, DeWitt and Lila Acheson Wallace concentrated their energies and pooled their resources for production of the crucial succeeding issues. To cut their living expenses to the minimum they sublet one room of their garden apartment in Greenwich Village to an instructor in New York University and his wife, sharing the bath and kitchen with their tenants. To save buying all the magazines they needed, DeWitt Wallace worked at the New York Public Library.

The periodical reading room was then on the Forty-second Street side of the main library on Fifth Avenue. Newspapers hung on racks, and a few magazines were on open shelves. Most of them could be obtained only by filing a slip with the librarian, who then had the copies brought from the stacks. The reading room was the haunt of derelicts from Bryant Park, who came in to escape the rain or snow and dozed in the warmth. Men and women out of jobs in the 1922 depression and without the money to buy a newspaper sidled guiltily in to check the newspaper help-wanted columns.

It was here Wallace worked, carefully selecting or rejecting articles in the current magazines. The articles he chose he laboriously condensed in longhand on sheets of yellow paper. He worked until his eyes blurred and his shoulders ached, slipped out to lunch, hurried back.

He might find something he wanted in the *Yale Review* in the morning, another possibility in *Physical Culture* that afternoon. He filed request slips at the same time for *The Saturday Evening Post, McClure's, Current History,* and *American Magazine, The Rotarian,* perhaps a few others. Sometimes he found nothing, sometimes pounced on a golden bit. His aunt had many times told him of the odd characters who frequented the Minneapolis library and of their ridiculous requests. Wallace noted with amusement, sometimes with irritation, that the New York librarians had spotted him for one of these eccentrics. When he could do no more in a day, he hurried back to Greenwich Village for the mail.

The mail was good. The first issue of The Reader's Digest had caught on. People wrote, some rapturously, of their pleasure and satisfaction. New subscriptions were coming in. Continued mailings of circular letters to selected lists were pulling well. Confidence began to dispel anxiety in Wallace. In the second issue, March 1922, the editors were able to announce elatedly: "The Reader's Digest is successful beyond all anticipations."

Readers were pleased with the article-a-day idea. They liked the condensed form, which made for quick and easy reading. They saw the selection of the best appearing in all the important magazines as both a unique service and a bargain. That the Digest was of small book size, meant to be kept, was still an added value. It was all reading matter, no advertising. At twenty-five cents a copy, three dollars for a year's subscription—price which was to remain unchanged until 1957—The Reader's Digest was a small but encouraging success.

The monthly wrapping and addressing of the Digests at 1 Minetta Lane, with girls from the community club hired each time to help, were exciting occasions, followed usually by celebrating over coffee and griddle cakes at a nearby Childs restaurant. Subscriptions came in so well that only once in the first five months was Wallace behind with his payments to the printer in Pittsburgh. A month later, because of shipping delays from Pittsburgh, printing was shifted to a plant in Floral Park on Long Island.

By fall of 1922 the Wallaces were in position to make another change they had hopefully contemplated. They wanted to get out of New York into the country where they could live and work without noise and distractions. A notice on the bulletin board at their garden apartment described a garage apartment available in Pleasantville in Westchester County. Mrs. Wallace had spent a summer there before her marriage. They had been married in a Pleasantville church. They hurried to Grand Central.

Pendleton Dudley, who had established his public-relations office in the New York financial district in 1907, was finishing a round of golf at the Nannahagen course in Pleasantville when the caddy master came across to the ninth green to tell him that a young man and woman were waiting to talk with him. DeWitt and Lila Acheson Wallace had seen his garage apartment and now wanted to know whether it had been rented yet and, if not, what the rent was.

Dudley saw them as an unusual couple, handsome, modest, but direct. They were publishing a magazine, they explained, and what they wanted was a place in which to live and work. Dudley, who knew something of the complex magazine business and the capital and organization usually involved, was startled.

"All by yourselves?"

All by themselves, the Wallaces assured him. Deciding that two young innocents embarked on such a project needed all the help they could get, Dudley told them they could set the rent at whatever they thought the place was worth to them. They agreed on $25 a month and, a little later, an additional $10 monthly for an unused pony shed, which had been built against one end of the garage, to use as an office for The Reader's Digest.

Dudley's was a two-car fieldstone garage in Dutch colonial design to match his hilltop, maple-shaded house. The upper story was shingled. There were dormers with casement windows. The apartment, about 25 by 30 feet, consisted of one long room with a huge fireplace at one end, a domed ceiling with exposed beams, and a bath and tiny kitchen at the other end. The Wallaces moved in as quickly as they could. It was a strange moving day. The Wallaces' furniture consisted almost wholly of bundles of magazines and stacks of letters. The Wallaces swept, scoured, painted the woodwork themselves, bought a minimum of furniture, and quickly went to work.

Dudley soon saw that he had distinctive tenants. Both DeWitt and Lila Acheson Wallace were capable of intense sustained effort. They were working purposefully in a glow of subdued excitement. At 33, DeWitt Wallace was a man moving with the certainty and determination of a man who had found what he wanted to do in life and was doing it. The Wallaces began work early in the morning and worked until late at night. So quickly had The Reader's Digest caught on that they now had 7000 subscribers and were gaining more with every issue. Besides seeing to it that the atmosphere was one in which DeWitt Wallace could work fiercely and happily, Lila Acheson Wallace read the current magazines and chose those pieces she thought best for Digest treatment. De Witt Wallace reviewed them and did most of the actual condensations, although Lila helped also in this area.

He wrote magazine editors, as he had from the first, asking for permission to reprint already published material. As these editors saw valuable publicity in the additional circulation given the articles with credit to their periodicals, it was permission they were happy to grant. Only one editor refused; George Horace Lorimer of *The Saturday Evening Post* had a long-standing rule forbidding quotation of more than 500 words. Wallace took a train for Philadelphia and persuaded the most powerful editor in the country to make the first exception he had ever made.

Between selecting and digesting the editors obtained new mailing lists and circularized them, writing their own promotional copy, addressing and stamping the envelopes, carting them themselves to the Pleasantville post office. For recreation Wallace pitched horseshoes or played at catch behind the garage with the frequent weekend guests to their tiny estate. Flowers blossomed in the window boxes in summer. Hollyhocks bloomed alongside the garage walls. Lila Acheson Wallace, Pendleton Dudley remembers, had the interior, with its great fireplace, delightfully furnished and arranged. The Wallaces were vital, gay, happy. All of the energy DeWitt Wallace had expended in sports and restlessness in earlier years was integrated now. Both of them were inherently interested in people, insatiably curious—qualities evident from the first in the Digest—but Wallace had already developed the habit of seeing and hearing only what interested him, and what interested him was The Reader's Digest.

As the magazine earned more money, the Wallaces would sometimes move to a country hotel or some rural lodging secure from interruption and, through concentrated effort, prepare a complete issue of the magazine from already selected material in a week or ten days. It left the rest of the month free for dealing with editors and working toward further increases in circulation. Wallace of his own volition did one other thing which proved later of great importance. As soon as he was able, he began to pay small sums to surprised magazine editors for the articles he chose, condensed, and reprinted.

Wallace had learned the fundamentals of promotion and learned them well with Webb, Brown & Bigelow, and Westinghouse. He hammered away relentlessly. Every issue contained his consistent, repeated appeals. As the Digest does today, he printed testimonials from enthusiastic subscribers. These were not the great of the world in those days but teachers, lawyers, doctors, housewives, most of whom expressed their greatest pleasure in the timesaving qualities of the Digest. Wallace stressed its handy size, its compactness, its permanence, its selection of articles of lasting interest. In August 1923 he was explaining and urging:

The Reader's Digest is not a magazine in the usual sense, but rather a co-operative means of rendering a timesaving service. Our Association is serving you; it should also be serving your friends.

The Reader's Digest Association had been formed with DeWitt Wallace owning 52 per cent of the stock, Lila Acheson Wallace the remaining 48 per cent. Subscribers became members of the Association.

Wallace offered low renewal rates to subscribers who obtained a number of new subscriptions. He made an "Extraordinary Announcement." A subscriber would receive a year's renewal subscription free if he sent in only one new yearly subscription at the full three-dollar price and merely the names of ten or more prospects. Issue after issue the Digest was writing by J. B. S. Haldane, Newell Dwight Hillis, Edwin Markham, Joseph Conrad, Ernest Poole, Courtney Ryley Cooper, Beatrice Forbes-Robertson Hale, and their scientific, religious, literary, journalistic, and dramatic fellows and counterparts—and tell your friends about The Reader's Digest service.

With the issue of September 1923 the idealized woman disappeared and the table of contents was shifted from the inside to the outside of the cover where, front or back, it has remained ever since. Under the logotype, reset in Old English, appeared the capitalized word, SERVICE. Occasionally the wording of the Digest's legend was slightly changed. It became in some early issues:

"AN ARTICLE A DAY" FROM LEADING MAGAZINES
—EACH ARTICLE OF ENDURING VALUE AND INTEREST,
IN CONDENSED, PERMANENT BOOKLET FORM.

The contents bore out the editors' contentions.

Among the writers in The Reader's Digest in 1922–23 were Harry Emerson Fosdick, Lincoln Steffens, Luther Burbank, Max Nordau, Donald Ogden Stewart, Dr. G. Stanley Hall, John Galsworthy, H. G. Wells, Bertrand Russell, Burton J. Hendrick, Lloyd C. Douglas, Gabriele d'Annunzio—popular preachers, crusading journalists, scientists, best-selling novelists, poets, humorists, naturalists, philosophers, economists.

Subjects covered included love, friendship, politics, morals, music, immigration, self-improvement. During the Digest's first year Harry Lauder, Louis Pasteur, Will Durant, Charles Schwab, Fielding Yost, all appeared either as article authors or subjects. Holworthy Hall (Harold C. Porter, who took his pen name from his Harvard dormitory) was in with "Keeping Your Friendships in Repair" from the *American Magazine* and Gutzon Borglum with "Moulding a Mountain" from the *Forum*. From the start Reader's Digest titles, often alliterative, always provocative, were bright as newly minted dimes.

Better Brains—or Bedlam
Barnum and the Birth Rate
The Art of Courtship
Seven Ways to Improve Your Memory
Nature's Inexorable Law—Inequality
The Fashionable Subconscious
What Is a Girl To Do?
Wooden Indian and Iron Door
Official Schools of Crime
What Is Marriage?
Insulin—Miracle of Science

At Christmas, 1923, the Digest offered a special rate of $2.75 for a one-year subscription or $2.50 each for two or more subscriptions. An "unprecedented offer" to subscribers was a year's extension of their subscriptions for obtaining ten new subscriptions. The editors were exhilarated by their swift success. The Digest itself was their best advertising, but they were leaving lit-

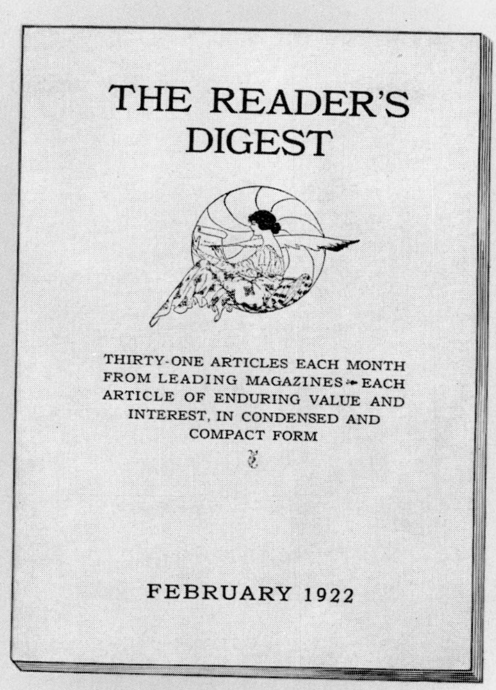
THE READER'S DIGEST

THIRTY-ONE ARTICLES EACH MONTH FROM LEADING MAGAZINES • EACH ARTICLE OF ENDURING VALUE AND INTEREST, IN CONDENSED AND COMPACT FORM

FEBRUARY 1922

Volume One, Number One of The Reader's Digest. A pocket-sized digest of articles reprinted from leading magazines, it contained the basic elements of The Reader's Digest today.

Published from a basement room at 1 Minetta Lane in the Greenwich Village section of Manhattan, the first 62-page issue of The Reader's Digest—black and white, unillustrated, containing no advertising—went hopefully to a list of 1500 trusting charter subscribers.

KARSH

DEWITT WALLACE

originator, founder and editor,
of The Reader's Digest

The Reader's Digest was the idea of one man, the joint venture of two people.

DeWitt Wallace, son of Dr. James Wallace, President of Macalester College in St. Paul, Minnesota, conceived the idea of a pocket-sized periodical which would digest articles of lasting interest from all the important magazines.

While recovering from wounds suffered in France during World War I, DeWitt Wallace practiced digesting articles of more than transient value from the leading American magazines. After discharge from the army he continued selecting and digesting magazine articles in the Minneapolis Public Library. In 1920 he printed a sample issue of The Reader's Digest.

Every publisher to whom he submitted the sample issue rejected the idea. When he was discharged from a job in Pittsburgh during the depression of 1921, DeWitt Wallace decided to try to publish the new magazine himself and began to circularize the public through the mails in an effort to obtain provisional subscribers.

DeWitt Wallace was joined in this effort by Lila Bell Acheson, to whom he had become engaged. They were married in the autumn of 1921. By borrowing a small sum to add to the amount

brought in by the subscriber appeals, they were able to launch the first Reader's Digest in February 1922. Their joint efforts have brought The Reader's Digest to its present multi-million world-wide circulation in many editions and many languages.

Fountain in the front entrance of Reader's Digest.

A dogwood-bordered walk at The Reader's Digest.

GOTTSCHO-SCHLEISNER

AVEDON

LILA ACHESON WALLACE

co-founder and co-editor,
of The Reader's Digest

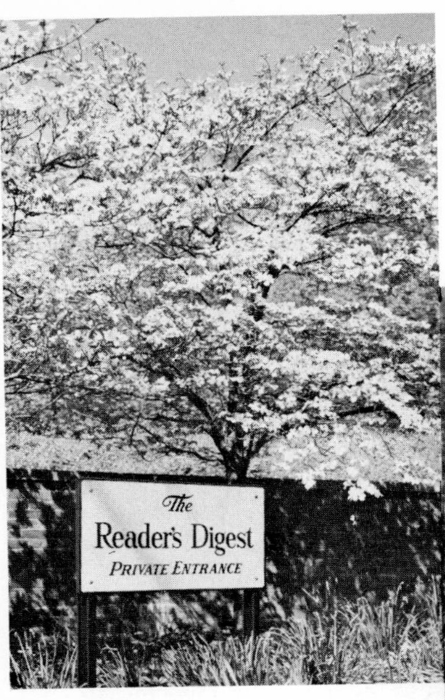

Sign at the entrance to the spacious grounds of The Reader's Digest editorial and circulation offices on Route 117 above Chappaqua, New York.

An aerial view of The Reader's Digest headquarters among the wooded hills of northern Westchester County. The growth of the magazine has necessitated sprawling additions to the original building erected in 1939.

CONTINENTAL AIR VIEWS

FORB

High Winds, home of DeWitt Wallace and Lila Acheson Wallace

Of Norman design, towered High Winds stands on 100 acres atop a steep hillside overlooking Byram Lake in Mt. Kisco, New York. The house, a few miles from The Reader's Digest editorial offices, is of native stone with pegged studding of timbers taken from ancient barns in the locality.

tle to chance. Every cent they could spare was going into circularizing. Their whole effort went into firming the foundation and strengthening the Digest structure. They planned for every contingency they could foresee.

DeWitt Wallace had had one of those ideas so simple that it is obvious to everyone once it has been pointed out and its validity proved. He had sensed that modern men and women preferred to read what was brief and clear. He believed that what appealed to him as writing of lasting interest would appeal to others. He had developed the ability to shorten articles, retain their substance, keep them accurate to their authors' intent, and at the same time enhance their readability.

Wallace could phrase now just what he was attempting. The first Digests carried substantial material drawn from a backlog of magazines over a number of years. Later Digests were limited to material selected from the current issues of the leading magazines. The first Digests had been directed primarily to teachers and professional men and women. There had been a deliberate effort to reach newly enfranchised, newly emancipated women readers—even to printing the names of two women, who had no actual part in the production of the magazine, on the masthead. The Wallaces were reaching now for the larger public which its mounting circulation showed that the Digest was already beginning to reach. Editorial aims were widened. DeWitt Wallace phrased the Digest intent now as the presentation of "articles of lasting interest which will appeal to a large audience, articles that come within the range of interests, experience, and conversation of the average person."

CHAPTER V

THE FIRST READER'S DIGEST ORIGINAL ARTICLES

The one contingency DeWitt Wallace and Lila Acheson Wallace could not foresee was the speed and, given its beginnings, the magnitude of The Reader's Digest's acceptance by the public.

Before the Wallaces had been three years in Pleasantville the burgeoning magazine threatened to burst the stone walls of the garage apartment and pony shed. In 1925 they bought land that had long been vacant next to Pendleton Dudley and built a home and office of their own. It was a long, low, Normandy house with oak-paneled stucco walls and a varicolored slate roof. "A jewel of a house," Dudley called it. It was a gracious place, but it delights Lila Acheson Wallace to remember that her mother admonished an exclaiming visitor with, "Oh, but you should have seen the garage!"

Also in 1925 the Wallaces hired, as "business manager," their first full-time employee, a young man who had journeyed to Pleasantville in search of a publishing job. Ralph Ernest Henderson, four years out of Harvard, was the Burma-born son of an American missionary. Henderson, now editor of The Reader's Digest Condensed Book Club, recalls that one of his duties then was to stuff the wrappers, addressed in Pleasantville, for the 16,500 press run of the Digest into the back of Wallace's Studebaker roadster and take them to the printer's on Long Island.

The Reader's Digest quickly outgrew even its new quarters. The Wallaces rented the upper floor and basement of the Pleasantville post office. The Digest spilled out of these, and they rented in addition two floors of a bank building, hiring local workers for their subscription and promotion work. More subscriptions than they could handle in these enlarged quarters poured in. The Wallaces rented three more floors in another bank building in Pleasantville.

One reason for the little magazine's tremendous growth was the circularizing, continued unceasingly and, when funds were available for the purpose, on a larger scale. A more fundamental reason lay in the contents of the Digest itself. People liked what they found and read in "the little magazine." The 1920s were enfevered by the restlessness and confusion which followed the first global war, the discovery of sex through the popularization of Freudian psychology, and the emancipation of everybody from everything. The lost generation bewailed its disillusion with romantic bitterness. Braying derision of tradition cut shrill through the jazz. "Victorian" was a term of contempt. The swashbuckling iconoclasm of H. L. Mencken was the delight of undergraduates, and Prohibition added thrill to gagging over bootleg gin. There was too much of everything too soon. The simplicity of The Reader's Digest, its appeal to the individual, its sanity and humor, its unified coverage, made the anarchy seem somewhat more intelligible and life supportable.

Digest circulation reached 20,000 in 1926 with gross receipts of $60,000 for the year. In 1928, when a representative came to

Pleasantville soliciting the business, printing of the Digest was shifted from Long Island to the big Rumford Press in Concord, New Hampshire, which published a list of other magazines. The Digest was soon its largest client. By 1929 circulation was 216,190 and the gross had multiplied ten times to $600,000. This was a far larger circulation than that of many of the magazines from which DeWitt Wallace was reprinting the "articles of lasting interest" with direct appeal to the average individual. The Digest was stronger financially than many of the older periodicals. It was a satisfying but, as DeWitt Wallace well knew, a dangerous position.

He had tested the Digest on newsstands in Cleveland and in Los Angeles in 1925, and the tests had proved that the magazine would sell as well single-copy as by subscription. He had not placed it on newsstand sale for two reasons. One reason was that the Digest was sold as a special service to subscribers. It would cease to be so regarded if subscribers saw it on the newsstands. The other and more important reason was that as soon as The Reader's Digest was placed generally on the newsstands its success would invite competition from publishers who had far greater financial resources than the Wallaces. There was the possibility, too, that the publishers of some of the magazines on which the Digest depended for material might look on The Reader's Digest as a formidable and fast-growing competitor.

In 1929 competition forced DeWitt Wallace to take the step he might have deferred longer. Imitators of the Digest appeared. These aped the page size, format, even the type style of The Reader's Digest. They had not the Digest's substance or spirit. Some simply pirated already published material without bothering to ask permission of the copyright holders. Most of these publications were short-lived, but they represented a potential danger. When one of them, *Fleet's Review,* appeared on the newsstands, DeWitt Wallace decided to add single-copy to subscription sales for The Reader's Digest.

The American News Company, then the magazine-distribution giant, refused to take on the Digest, contending that it had no circulation potential on the newsstands. Wilbert Smith, president of S-M News, who had read and liked the Digest, wrote DeWitt Wallace, soliciting the Digest as a client. S-M had been founded as a distributing organization in 1919 by *Popular Science Monthly* and *McCall's Magazine.* Wallace promptly closed with S-M, which still distributes the Digest. S-M placed 100,000 copies of the April 1929 issue of The Reader's Digest on the newsstands and sold 62,000 of them. The S-M connection was to have an added importance for the Digest. President of *Popular Science* in 1929 and a vice-president of S-M was A. L. Cole. Cole, one of the ablest circulation men in magazine publishing, became business adviser to the Digest in 1932 and since 1939 has been its general business manager.

Though its newsstand appearance and sale divulged the stature which the Digest had now achieved, most editors, convinced that republication of their articles in The Reader's Digest stimulated mass readership of quality writing, continued to allow DeWitt Wallace the reprint rights for which he was now able to pay liberally. *Scribner's* refused to renew its reprint privileges, fearing that the Digest was cutting into its own circulation. The *Atlantic Monthly* and the *Forum* threatened to sever relationships.

DeWitt Wallace thereupon instituted contracts with his more important source publications under which he paid a blanket fee for the exclusive right to reprint for a stated period an article a month in The Reader's Digest. Lengths of the contracts varied. The undivulged sums paid also varied by circulation and importance to the Digest of the contracting magazine. Most of the leading magazines were glad to agree to an arrangement which brought them not only financial reward, but also a larger magazine-reading public. The *American, The Saturday Evening Post,* and the Hearst magazines demurred, then quickly followed the lead of the majority. Soon The Reader's Digest, which had grown from its original 64 pages to 128 pages each issue, held exclusive reprint agreements with thirty-five of the leading American magazines, including those which had threatened to withdraw.

DeWitt Wallace was faced with another danger. Some of the well-known magazines from which he had been able to cull articles suitable for condensation in the early issues of The Reader's Digest had already disappeared. Others, he knew, were in shaky financial condition. Radio, motion pictures, the increased use of the automobile, simple competition, had killed off the weaker publications, and more were going to succumb during the severe economic depression which had already started. Thirty-five or forty of the leading magazines which Wallace found fruitful sources of Digest material in the 1920s have long since vanished. *The North American Review, Scribner's,* the *Century, Review of Reviews, Hearst's International,* the *Forum, World's Work, McClure's,* the *American, Collier's, Current History, Judge,* the old *Life,* the *Delineator, Pictorial Review, Woman's Home Companion, Mentor*—to mention but a few of the better known—are all defunct. The Wallaces could no longer be sure of obtaining all the material they needed from other magazines.

The move toward creating original material for publication in

The Reader's Digest was thus, in a sense, precautionary. In a strongly individualistic magazine which had already begun to establish its own tone and character it was, in another sense, inevitable.

Until he could gauge his readers' reactions, DeWitt Wallace went about the change very slowly. In 1930 The Reader's Digest was condensing articles of significance from publications as varied as the *New Republic, Vanity Fair, Liberty, Plain Talk, The Christian Science Monitor, Virginia Quarterly Review, American Mercury,* the *Theatre Guild Magazine, The New Yorker, Christian Century, Business Week Survey,* the *New Freeman, Sportsman,* even *Chambers's Journal of Edinburgh,* the *Illustrated London News,* and *The Tatler and American Sketch.* In April 1930 came an article attributed to no source publication. "Music and Work," unsigned, was described as "a special compilation for The Reader's Digest." "Music and Health" followed in May. In June "Music and Animals" was described as "a summary especially prepared by one of our editors." In July 1930 there was another unsigned original, "The Worker Practices a New Art"—the new art was the drama as performed by workers' groups in various parts of the United States and abroad.

The October 1931 issue of the Digest opened with an unsigned Digest original, "Paging Coolidge, Smith, Baker, and Dawes," an appeal to recall to service out-of-office public men of proved accomplishment to help solve the worsening economic crisis.

The first signed original article in The Reader's Digest appeared in February 1933. It was "Insanity—The Modern Menace" by Henry Morton Robinson. It was followed in March with a nature piece by Archibald Rutledge, "Animals in Sleep." Rutledge was back in April with "America's Kindliest Race," and the same issue carried another signed Digest original, "Gambling Government," by Henry Kittredge Norton. Signed articles by Charles W. Ferguson, Frank R. Kent, and Francis Rufus Bellamy followed during the year.

At the same time another type of Digest original was developed. These are articles which, written on Digest assignment, are then offered to, accepted by, published in, and then condensed from other magazines. Many magazines, some general, some technical or specialized, do not have funds available to command the best writers or carry on the often extensive research which goes into the preparation of a Reader's Digest article. When an article which seems to fit the editorial needs of one of these magazines is written for The Reader's Digest, the editor of that magazine is asked if he is interested. If, exercising the same editorial freedom and judgment he employs on other manuscripts submitted, he accepts the article, it is then published in full in his magazine, the Digest paying the writer for the original manuscript. It is then republished in condensed form in The Reader's Digest.

There are numerous advantages to the writer, the magazine which first publishes the material, and to the Digest. For one thing, the Digest is often able to add the research facilities of a specialized publication to its own in the preparation and checking of an article. A medical journal can lend its research facilities for a medical article; a scientific publication or a journal of the arts does the same for a subject in its fields of interest.

The writer of the article has the satisfaction of seeing his uncut version in print. The magazine accepting the article has the double advantage of running an article normally beyond its means and seeing its name listed—a demonstrated asset—in the Digest's table of contents. The Digest benefits from being able to make an acceptable condensation on its usual pattern from an already published full-length article. The Digest made candid acknowledgment of this practice from its inception. DeWitt Wallace regards the magazine's article-placement policy as "one of the best things the Digest ever did and a source of pride to all of us."

The Wallaces knew which Digest articles had produced the greatest and most favorable response among their readers. They were aware that the Digest's appeal rested on something more than the skillful condensation of its varied material. Much more than for their brevity, Digest articles had come to be recognized for their wide range of interests, the warmth of their appeal, their personal and optimistic approach, their simple reality. This they saw as the unique editorial contribution and province of The Reader's Digest. Digest originals were initiated as a means of further improving and developing that contribution.

DeWitt Wallace saw the move as "an inevitable development, perhaps the most important in the Digest's history. Far from marking a change in the Digest's editorial formula, this, in fact, was a means to strengthen and extend it.

"Through our familiarity with the Digest's growing audience, we came to have a pretty clear picture of what our readers expected from us, the kind of article that interested and meant the most to them. We were positive that, better than anyone on the outside, we could plan such articles, find the writers best qualified to produce them, and thereby insure more of the kind of articles which our readers recognized as distinctively Reader's Digest.

"We were also sure that, by the ability of our editors in abbreviation and condensation, we could make the work of qualified writers more readable while, at the same time, preserving the style, spirit, and substance of their articles as originally written. As a result, the development of original articles became a major Digest policy just as soon as the magazine's growth justified the additional editorial expense."

An original Reader's Digest article, published in August 1935, only two years after the Digest began the use of signed pieces, has become famous as perhaps the most successful, widely circulated, read, and talked-about magazine article ever published. It did much to bring the Digest to even wider public notice, accelerated its already swift circulation growth. Far beyond all that, it struck the public consciousness with harsh and strong impact, focusing sharp attention on a national tragedy.

DeWitt Wallace, driving about the Pleasantville countryside one afternoon, remembered accidents he had read about, others he had seen. Following his train of thought, he stopped at a garage in Armonk and asked its owner whether he had had any bad wrecks brought in lately. The garage man had. He described some accidents he had seen at length and in gruesome detail. As Wallace said later, "He told me plenty!" Quickly Wallace got in touch with J. C. Furnas, who was working on an article on traffic problems for the Digest, told him to drop it and to start immediately to work on a short, hard-hitting article which would dramatize the necessity of safer driving. It was Wallace's intent to shock the country into realization of the thousands of highway tragedies, many of them due to reckless or careless driving, that were happening everywhere. Deliberately he planned an article so grimly realistic that it would penetrate public indifference.

The result was "—And Sudden Death." It was a grisly piece—blood, bones protruding through torn flesh, corpses strewn about the road, bodies smashed beyond recognition. No effort was made to spare the reader. The article was written and rewritten before the editors were satisfied that it had the brutal qualities they wanted it to have.

The article was set with an italicized editorial warning preceding it:

> *Like the gruesome spectacle of a bad automobile accident itself, the realistic details of this article will nauseate some readers. Those who find themselves thus affected at the outset are cautioned against reading the article in its entirety, since there is no letdown in the author's outspoken treatment of sickening fact.*

There was no letdown. The article, as it said it would in its opening paragraph, translated "dry statistics into a reality of blood and agony." It commented that even "a mangled body on a slab, waxily portraying the consequences of bad motoring judgment, isn't a patch on the scene of the accident itself." The piece went on to describe what it said that no artist working on a safety poster would dare depict in full detail—"the flopping, pointless efforts of the injured to stand up; the queer, grunting noises; the steady, panting groaning of a human being with pain creeping up on him as the shock wears off . . . the slack expression of a man, drugged with shock, staring at the Z-twist in his broken leg, the insane crumpled effect of a child's body . . ."

All the pain, horror, and savage mutilation of a bad automobile accident were hurled full into the reader's face. It was a forceful article, perhaps too forceful. It could hurt the Digest, but it might do some good. A proof of it in his hand, DeWitt Wallace walked across the lawn between their two houses and asked Pendleton

Dudley if he wanted to publicize it. Once he had seen the unyielding brutality of the piece and grasped its nationwide implications, experienced Dudley knew at once that it could be successfully publicized.

It was. Proofs were sent to 5000 newspapers and other publications with invitations to reprint the article after it had appeared in the Digest. It was reprinted in whole or in part in newspapers in every large American city. Weeklies, farm and religious papers, company house organs gave it additional circulation. As far as Pendleton Dudley's organization was able to discover—and it has handled all Digest publicity since that time—quotations from news releases and editorials appeared in American newspapers virtually without exception.

"—And Sudden Death," timely and terrible, was read and discussed on radio programs, made the subject of formal discussions in the programs of civic clubs. It was syndicated as a comic strip, made into a short motion picture. Traffic-court judges read it aloud in crowded courtrooms. Magistrates made offenders on traffic charges copy it in longhand. Reprints were mailed with all official correspondence of the Province of Ontario. Wyoming packed copies with every set of license plates issued. New York handed reprints to motorists going through the Holland Tunnel or over the George Washington Bridge.

Within three months The Reader's Digest distributed 4,000,000 reprints of "—And Sudden Death" to more than 8000 companies, clubs, civic groups, and other associations which requested them, giving the article greater circulation than any other magazine article before or since. One investigator, who kept records for several months after the Digest's original publication of the article, found a noticeable decrease in the number of highway accidents following its appearance. All of the improvement certainly cannot be attributed to "—And Sudden Death," but in 1935 automobiles were killing 13 people a year for every 10,000 cars in use. In the next six years the ratio of traffic deaths to miles driven declined by one-third.

Paul Hoffman, who in 1935 was vice-president in charge of sales for the Studebaker Corporation, was also at that time chairman of the Safety Committee of the Automobile Manufacturers Association. The committee, he says, met once a year, issued a publicity release, and did little else. Hoffman had been deeply interested in automotive safety for years. He had earlier been active chairman of the first traffic commission in Los Angeles. Like other executives of the automobile industry, he had simply got so busy with the everyday problems of selling cars that he had little time left to think about highway safety.

His committee of the Automobile Manufacturers Association, Hoffman believes, might have continued in this state of indifference had it not been for the publication of "—And Sudden Death." "The public furor caused by that article," Paul Hoffman told the graduating class of the Traffic Institute at Northwestern University in 1956, "frightened us into action. We decided that producing and selling more and better automobiles wasn't enough—it was up to the industry to contribute what it could to making highway travel safer and more efficient."

Hoffman put his moribund safety committee to work. Out of its study came formation of the Automotive Safety Foundation, which has spent millions of dollars since its inception in supporting the work of traffic-safety organization.

The influence of the Furnas article has been as lasting as its initial appearance was spectacular. It added to the reputation of the magazine which conceived and developed the story and published it at a time when the inclusion of original material in its pages was comparatively new and full implications of the step could not yet be known. "—And Sudden Death" became the first of the many Reader's Digest originals with a public service as well as a circulation purpose.

CHAPTER VI

THE FIRST CONDENSED BOOKS

With the introduction of original articles into The Reader's Digest in the 1930s came also the introduction of original Reader's Digest departments, humorous, human-interest departments, which marked the beginning of reader participation as contributors to the magazine.

In February 1930 appeared "Repartee." Readers were invited to submit examples of witty riposte and rejoinder by well-known persons. Five dollars was paid for each accepted. "Repartee" closed after a few months. "Origins" was started in March 1930. This department paid five dollars to successful contributors for descriptions of the unusual origins of words. It too soon closed. The trouble was that most of the definitions were unusual enough, but that few of them were authentic.

"Patter" ran in most issues during 1931 and 1932. This was two or three pages of jokes from various published sources. A department that was to last much longer under a slightly changed and now widely familiar title was started in the Digest for September 1931 as "The Well-Known Human Race." Again reader contributions were sought at five dollars for each acceptance. Soon came "Quotable Quotes," "Picturesque Speech," "Toward a More Picturesque Speech," "Pert and Pertinent," and "Boners." Some of these departments still survive. Others developed into such famous Reader's Digest departments as "Life in These United States," "Drama in Real Life," and "The Most Unforgettable Character I've Met." The addition of these departments with the addition of original Digest articles intensified the peculiar appeal of The Reader's Digest. They became as much a part of the magazine as the wide coverage and the brevity and simplicity of article treatment which DeWitt Wallace had foreseen would appeal to a faster-moving, fact-hungry postwar generation.

Continuing scrutiny of other publications produced significant and enduring Digest pieces from an ever-wide variety of magazines—*Time,* the *McGill News, American Scholar, Spur, Acadia, San Quentin Bulletin, Liberty, Country Gentleman, The Bookman,* the *Golden Book, Maclean's, Technology Review, American Boy.* At the same time editorial expenditures for Digest originals were increased on the assumption, amply proved, that the Digest's best promotion was articles planned and written exclusively for the Reader's Digest audience.

Every successful magazine develops its own character. It becomes a distinct and recognizable entity. It will remain as complex as an individual human being but, like the individual, be consistently itself and different from any other magazine. Usually this is true because the magazine reflects the temperament and character, the limitations and the reach of the mind, emotions, and imagination of its distinct editor. *Godey's Lady's Book* was Sarah Josepha Hale. The *American Mercury* was H. L. Mencken. *The Saturday Evening Post* was once essentially George Horace Lorimer, just as *The New Yorker* was Harold

Ross. With the publication of original articles and departments, The Reader's Digest reflected more directly the characteristics, tastes, and opinions of its editors. Creativeness was added to the critical skill exercised in selecting and condensing articles from other published sources. As a result, The Reader's Digest took on stature and firm identity transcending that given it by its unique pocket size and its distinctiveness as a reprint magazine.

A third major change in the contents of The Reader's Digest came at the end of 1934. Toward the back of the Christmas issue there was this notice:

> *With each passing year for more than a decade, the editors of The Reader's Digest have sought to enlarge the magazine's scope and to enhance the vitality of its interest and usefulness.*
>
> *In furtherance of this policy, the present issue has been increased from 112 to 128 pages, to permit publication of an extensive condensation from a suitable book. The magazine remains otherwise unaltered.*
>
> *Readers' comments and suggestions, which have always given helpful guidance to the growth of the magazine, will be particularly welcome in connection with this new step.*

Following this announcement was a condensation of Arnold Bennett's *How To Live on Twenty-four Hours a Day*. It was described as "a little classic in the science of self-direction, suggesting an infallible antidote to mental flabbiness—a technique which assures adding zest to all one's daily activity."

Actually The Reader's Digest had run a brief condensation of Bennett's book 12 years earlier. A shorter version had appeared in the second issue of the magazine, March 1922. In the years 1922–33 there had been nearly 100—92, by count—short book condensations, though most of these had been condensations of parts or chapters rather than of entire volumes. The Digest pioneered in the use of condensed nonfiction book material, using the work of such contrasting writers as Gelett Burgess, Edward Bok, Sir James Jeans, Robert Benchley, Stuart Chase, Robert Ripley, James Truslow Adams, Stephen Leacock, Mary Beard, Stefan Zweig, Clare Boothe Brokaw, Hendrik Van Loon, Lowell Thomas, Ogden Nash, and Lafcadio Hearn. It had condensed pieces from such books as *Jean-Christophe, The Mysterious Universe, The Epic of America, The Paradox of Plenty,* and others all the way from J. Arthur Thomson's *The Outline of Science* to Will Cuppy's *How to Tell Your Friends from the Apes,* Ernest Dimnet's *The Art of Thinking,* and Pitkin's *Life Begins at Forty.*

The 1934 condensation of *How To Live on Twenty-four Hours a Day*—the Digest reprinted it in April 1958—introduced what has been an outstanding feature of the magazine since that time and one which presaged the inauguration of The Reader's Digest Condensed Book Club 16 years later. Bennett's book was followed in later Digests by Norman Archibald's *Heaven High—Hell Deep,* Clifford Beers' *A Mind That Found Itself,* Irving Stone's *Lust for Life,* and other popular books, and the condensed book took its place beside the condensed article in the Digest. Some book publishers, fearful that Digest condensation might injure their sales, demurred at first. When in 1936 DeWitt Wallace offered Harper's $1000 for the rights to reprint 50 pages condensed from Alexis Carrel's *Man the Unknown,* the offer was refused on these grounds. Wallace countered with a wager. If sales of the book did not increase instead of decline after Digest condensation, he would pay the publisher $5000 instead of $1000. Sales of *Man the Unknown* promptly quadrupled after the Digest's condensation. Wallace paid only the $1000, a liberal figure at the time.

Almost invariably condensation of a book in The Reader's Digest has led to a wider audience for the complete work. *The Anatomy of Peace* by Emory Reeves, which the Digest condensed in three installments in 1945 and 1946, was known until then by comparatively few readers. Copies lay undisturbed on the booksellers' shelves. Sales went to 100,000 after the book's appearance in the Digest. *A Man Called Peter* was already selling 6000 copies a week when the Digest condensed and reprinted it, but the month following, sales of the book leaped to 39,000, making it number one on the best-seller list.

With the addition of the condensed book the changes which both intensified the salient characteristics of the original Digest and gave the magazine the essential structure it has today were completed. Certain dangers had been successfully averted, and strong advances had been made.

The conscienceless tactics of the swarm of Reader's Digest imitators could have annoyed editors and publishers to the point where they would reject the whole idea of condensed reprints without discriminating between The Reader's Digest and the spoilers. Disclosure of Digest circulations when it went on the newsstands could have caused them to decide against continuing relations with an actual or potential competitor. Publication of original articles and condensed books in The Reader's Digest might have produced the same result.

Instead the Digest emerged tempered, strengthened, and formed, a strong and vigorous magazine in its own right. In 1936, with its circulation pushing 2,000,000, The Reader's Digest had an editorial staff of 32 in Pleasantville. A detail of three researchers was stationed at the New York Public Library. Another staff of ten women worked at the Cleveland Public Library, where open shelves made published material more readily available.

The Digest had firm exclusive reprint contracts with the leading magazines. For every monthly issue of the Digest its growing staff was examining a general list of some 200 weekly and monthly magazines and about 300 trade journals, scientific publications, and house organs. In addition to articles selected and condensed from these other periodicals and to signed originals by its own writers, the Digest was developing from five to ten originals every month to place with other magazines for later condensation and publication in its own pages.

Wallace was bringing to Pleasantville as Digest editors men who shared or reflected his own idealism, humor, and faith in human nature. Like Ralph Henderson, the Digest's first staff member, a number of these, including M. T. Ragsdale, Harry H. Harper, Cuyler McRae, George Ernest Grant, and a few years later Hobart Lewis, had had no previous editorial experience. Walter B. Mahony, Jr., now a senior editor, joined the Digest within a year after his graduation from college. Others of the new editors, like Howard Florance, who had served on both the *Review of Reviews* and the *Literary Digest,* were skilled journalists of wide newspaper and magazine experience.

Possibly in recompense for the days when he had been able to pay first nothing, then little, Wallace was paying generous to fabulous amounts of money to other magazines for reprint privileges, to writers working on Digest assignments, and to his key workers. He was making available quality articles by ranking authors to magazines of high literary and intellectual quality, which could not attempt to produce them independently. Some 60 of these Digest originals had already appeared in such magazines as the *Atlantic Monthly, Scribner's,* the *Forum, American Mercury, Today,* and *The North American Review* when, in November 1936, *Fortune* published a full-dress article on The Reader's Digest. It was no secret, *Fortune* pointed out, that this Digest support meant all the difference between failure and solvency for some magazines of the highest standards and repute.

The Digest could no longer remain unnoticed in the rural quiet of northern Westchester. It had sprung into unsought prominence as a publishing phenomenon. Fantastic rumors about The Reader's Digest already swirled through New York magazine, book, and advertising circles. DeWitt Wallace, "shy, soft-voiced, embarrassed, generally ill at ease with strangers," had quietly originated and developed a unique periodical which already had a larger circulation than that of any other magazine without fiction or pictures. He had proved, said *Fortune,* that "if all reprint rights were withdrawn, he could produce a first-rate magazine of original articles, plus book condensations, and bright fillers."

DeWitt Wallace had done more. He had retained and strengthened the Digest's original identity as a magazine offering condensed reprints of the best articles published in all the other magazines, at the same time broadened and deepened The Reader's Digest by giving it unmistakable individuality and stature of its own.

CHAPTER VII

THE DIGEST'S CHAPPAQUA HEADQUARTERS

By 1936 The Reader's Digest, which had first overflowed Pendleton Dudley's stone garage and pony shed, then the new home and office of its owners, was overflowing the whole of the village of Pleasantville. The work of the magazine was being carried on in 14 separate and crowded offices scattered about the town. Though subscribers' copies and allotments to wholesalers and distributors were sent direct from the Rumford Press in Concord, New Hampshire, mailings of editorial and promotional material had brought the Pleasantville post office to first-class status.

DeWitt Wallace and the editors and writers he gathered about him as the Digest sprang from David to Goliath size worked in unmarked, cramped offices on the top floor of a bank building. On schedule, trains of the New York Central roared by beneath their windows. Lila Acheson Wallace, still very much an editor of the Digest, worked at home. Business executives of the Digest had their offices atop Pleasantville's other bank. There were few places in Pleasantville where the hundreds of Digest clerical employees could eat lunch. There were neither public nor private parking places adequate for their cars. The Digest was paying up to $60 a day in fines for workers forced to leave their cars on the streets. The need for more practical quarters was imperative.

A move into New York City was contemplated. It was estimated that rental or purchase of a building in the country's publishing center would save The Reader's Digest at least a quarter million dollars a year. The Wallaces preferred northern Westchester for themselves and their workers and as an atmosphere in which to edit and publish their magazine. As a result, the decision was made to purchase and build on 80 acres of land in a wooded area of rolling hills seven miles north of Pleasantville between Chappaqua and Mt. Kisco.

Harry G. Wilcox, now assistant secretary of The Reader's Digest Association in charge of maintenance and personnel—with additional duties that make him actually a sort of headquarters commandant—was a General Motors engineer, trained at Union College, whom the Wallaces had hired in 1930. Engaged at first in solving problems of shipping and transport, he acted later as owner's agent in the construction of High Winds, a new home which the Wallaces built in Mt. Kisco.

After the Digest had acquired land at Lawrence Farms, the Wallaces gave Wilcox new instructions, which he still remembers: "Put up a building. Let us know when it is ready and we'll move in."

Lila Acheson Wallace delighted in the architecture of restored colonial Williamsburg, Virginia. At Digest instigation, architects visited Williamsburg and on their return drew up plans inspired by the Capitol, the Governor's Palace, and the Wren Building of the College of William and Mary. Working with real-estate men, lawyers, architects, and contractors, Wilcox again served as owner's agent in the building of the Digest's new offices.

In 1939 the Digest moved into a white-towered, three-story, red-brick Georgian structure costing—in 1939 dollars—$1,500,-000 and affording in its 185,000 cubic feet of working space all the grace, charm, and comfort the Wallaces were able to devise. Since that time the growth of the Digest has necessitated three major additions and many extensions connected by a maze of passageways. The grounds have been extended by large additional acreage.

Mrs. Wallace has been responsible for both the interior decoration and the landscaping of the Digest's grounds. The editorial offices on the ground floor of the original building are furnished like studies in unusually well-appointed private homes. Traditional mahogany and walnut desks with inlaid leather tops, tables and cabinets, colorful carpeting, brightly upholstered divans, and easy chairs are to be found in most of them. Only four of the principal offices are furnished with original antiques. The others contain authentic reproductions carefully chosen to carry out the general scheme. DeWitt Wallace's office has a formal fireplace set into its paneled walls and flanked by deep leather chairs. In it hangs Marc Chagall's "The Three Candles." In Lila Acheson Wallace's office are the three pastel panels of Pierre Bonnard's "Stage Design."

The two paintings are part of the notable Reader's Digest Collection of Fine Arts, paintings mostly of the French impressionists and moderns which Mrs. Wallace acquired over a long period, choosing each picture, as she says, "for the joy in it."

A Utrillo and a Van Gogh hang in the Digest's reception room; another Utrillo is in the office of A. L. Cole, where there are also a Soutine and a Blatas. Georges Braque's "Sun Flowers," Blatas's "La Place au Ceret," and Redon's "Pegasus" all hang in the hall at the Digest, as does Modigliani's "Mme. Hebuterne." Other parts of the Digest Collection are at High Winds, the Wallaces' home in Mt. Kisco. Matisse, Bonnard, Monet, Manet, Degas, Renoir, and Toulouse-Lautrec all hang at High Winds, though occasionally one or several canvases may be on loan. They have been borrowed for exhibitions in the United States, in France, and in England, for the Edinburgh Festival, and sometimes by the artists themselves for showing in exhibitions of their own. Though none were acquired as investments, most of the paintings in the Reader's Digest Collection have increased greatly in value.

The main entrance at The Reader's Digest opens on a central rotunda paneled in pale green. Off it is a reception room with a selection of current magazines but also old books in fine bindings, its paintings, and fine period furniture. Freshly cut flowers are placed here daily—there is even a small room off the rotunda especially equipped for flower arranging. The editorial library is paneled in rare butternut wood, distinctively carved.

Some of the effects she wished Mrs. Wallace obtained by having the factory spray stock traditional pieces in the colors she specified. Furniture manufacturers found this arrangement so satisfactory that subsequently they made it standard operating procedure. Scattered throughout the Digest buildings are 25 lounges, most of them for the use of Digest women employees. There is a South Sea Lounge, a Garden Lounge, a Men's Fire House, a Pink Shell Lounge, each with its own special motif. These lounges carry point beyond their attractive appearance. Mrs. Wallace had the employee lounges so decorated and furnished that there is nothing in these rooms which Digest women employees cannot duplicate themselves in decorating and furnishing rooms in their own homes. The furniture and pictures are all copies of good originals. The rugs or carpeting are within the scope of a modest household budget. The Digest will even supply the formulae for the decorator paints used in these rooms to those who wish to duplicate the colors.

Outside the Digest the scene is pastoral and idyllic. Only the white cupola of the original building with the four figures of Pegasus—chosen by Mrs. Wallace as the symbol of The Reader's Digest—at its base is visible from New York Highway 117, which winds between Chappaqua and Mt. Kisco, then on up to Katonah and beyond. All the rest of the sprawling Digest headquarters is tucked behind a gentle rise amid fields and low stone walls. The backdrop is a line of wooded hills cutting across the expensively tailored landscape of residential northern Westchester. A discreet small sign in masthead lettering at the entrance to the sweeping drive is all that indicates that this is The Reader's Digest rather than another Westchester estate, or possibly a small New England college. The only other sign visible on the road is just south of the Digest's gates. It says, "Deer Crossing," making its own comment on the character of the countryside.

A tall oak spreads its branches before the main entrance. Full-grown oaks and beeches, sprayed with paraffin to retain their moisture, were moved in and set in place despite 90-degree summer temperatures. There are wide parking lots screened by strategic plantings and there are formal gardens on the Digest's grounds, but the rural atmosphere has been carefully preserved. Tons and tons of earth have been moved to achieve its unspoiled aspect. Hay is cut in summer on the rolling approaches through which the Digest has built the private roads which it also maintains. Fruit clings in autumn to apple trees planted on a knoll close to the main entrance. The orchard too was moved in full-grown. One day it was not there. The next it was. The Reader's Digest has received a national award for industrial landscaping.

Except at eight-thirty in the morning, when its roads are packed with private cars and buses bringing Digest people to work, and at four in the afternoon, when the Digest closes for the day, it is country-quiet and still about the Digest grounds. Soft music is piped into the offices at certain hours of the day. A modern cafeteria serves meals considerably below cost to all Digest employees, and there are special dining rooms in which editors and business executives of the Digest can hold luncheon conferences with writers, publishers, correspondents, businessmen, or members of the Digest's own overseas staffs. Some of these stay at the Digest's guesthouse, a perfectly restored 180-year-old farmhouse which stands, tall-pillared, behind a high hemlock hedge on a knoll just inside the Digest's gates. The house, exquisitely decorated under Mrs. Wallace's direction, is furnished with fine antiques of her choosing. The guesthouse, which somehow blends dignity, elegance, and homely comfort—from the antique Kirman in the formal living room to the shoebrushes in the guestroom closets—has its own domestic staff.

Dukes and duchesses, motion-picture stars, American and foreign statesmen, Nobel prize winners, the editors of most large American magazines and many small ones, book publishers, advertising-agency executives, many of the great and near great of the world, have visited the headquarters of The Reader's Digest in Chappaqua. So have thousands of high-school and college students and just Digest readers from every part of the country and many places abroad. One page of the guest book in the rotunda reception room recently showed visitors from Lima, Havana, Bombay, Mexico City, Hong Kong, Caracas, Chicago, Calcutta, Glasgow, Paris, Port-au-Prince. Helsinki, Bangkok, and Rio de Janiero are apt to appear on any day along with entries from New York, Poughkeepsie, Los Angeles, Scottsdale, Princeton, or Ashtabula. People are curious to know whence The Reader's Digest emanates.

Most leave delighted with what they have seen. Some are visibly disconcerted and a few frankly unbelieving. This is the place, the scene, the atmosphere where the most widely circulated and read magazine anywhere originates. Here have been written some of the words and here have been edited all of the articles they have seen at home, whether home is in the United States, Europe, South America, Asia—wherever it is. That quiet optimism and gentle humor, folk tales, and earthy inspiration could come out of such a setting is understandable. That vigorous exposés and research-documented attacks which have caused uproars in business, labor, government and brought shrill recrimination out of Madison Avenue or Washington or well-organized pressure groups, as well as out of communist countries have also originated here is not as easy to understand. Some of the most thoroughly incredulous visitors are those familiar with the metropolitan settings and tense atmosphere in which many other mass-circulation periodicals are produced.

The answer, as it must, lies with people. It lies with DeWitt Wallace and the editors and writers who help form and shape each issue of The Reader's Digest. It is who they are, what they are like, how they think and feel, how they utilize their skills and to what ends that make The Reader's Digest what it is. Here the obvious has specific point, for it is people rather than objects or abstract ideas, people as individuals rather than as national, political, or even social groups, that are the Digest's chief concern.

CHAPTER VIII

LIFE AT THE READER'S DIGEST

The affronted communist would find the several thousand clerical employees of The Reader's Digest deluded wage slaves abused by capitalism of the worst kind. The pure socialist, even some of the impure, can find a distasteful paternalism rampant at Chappaqua. Almost anyone else is staggered by the unusual environs, generous wages, complex of "other considerations," and the simple but rare human kindness that prevails in what must be one of the most unusual places of business in the United States. The statement is safe—and it has been made by gratified and sometimes incredulous employees and admiring to horrified observers alike—that there is no other place quite like it.

Faced with indisputable evidence, DeWitt and Lila Acheson Wallace have had to concede, however reluctantly, that The Reader's Digest has become a world-wide enterprise necessitating a large and complicated clerical operation, but they want to feel, and want their employees to feel, that it is still a small, friendly organization. They do everything they can to strengthen and maintain that belief.

There is a practical side to it. The Digest operates in a thin labor market. Near no center of large population, it must depend on the countryside for its base force and for the added seasonal help it needs and cannot always get in sufficient numbers during peak periods. Because of a lack of adequate public transport, it has had to subsidize and charter its own buses to transport its workers who live scattered from the New York City line north into Putnam County, east to Connecticut, and west to the Hudson River. Twenty-two of these buses bring Digest workers, 90 per cent of them women and 75 per cent of them married, down from Danbury, Brewster, Lake Mahopac, and Peekskill, up from Mt. Vernon, Yonkers, and White Plains, across from Ossining and Tarrytown and most of the Westchester villages en route, and return them to their homes in late afternoon. "It's not entirely unselfish of us to want to do things to attract and keep good employees," a personnel booklet, "You and The Reader's Digest," admits, but the Digest does considerably more than strict economic self-interest requires.

Working hours at the Digest are from 8:30 A.M. to 4 P.M., for the Wallaces believe that, like themselves, their workers want to enjoy the pleasures of the countryside in which they all live. There is a 35-minute break for lunch, served in the Digest's cafeteria. Holidays are numerous, 11 paid holidays during the year, and vacation plans are generous in the extreme. A worker who starts in January or February gets one week's paid vacation the first year, three weeks the next, four weeks thereafter. Because the Wallaces believe it desirable for an editor to travel abroad as well as in the United States, a dozen or more of the Digest's top editors get vacations of some six weeks to two months annually. During the summer months employees get in addition an occasional Friday so that the entire staff may have a long weekend. On request, workers may get their vacation pay in advance.

There are rest periods morning and afternoon, and every day there are the delights of the Digest's quarters inside and the lawns, gardens, and spacious landscaped grounds outside. "We have fresher air and more sunshine and, we believe, pleasant surroundings and better working conditions, more liberal vacation policies, etc., than you can find most places," says the same booklet. But it very practically continues, "We do not want you to feel we are trying to pay you in fresh air or sunshine. We realize that your pay check is the big thing to you."

That pay, based on area-rate surveys and job-evaluation tests, is high. Provided their work is satisfactory, employees hired at the minimum rate for a job are guaranteed a pay increase at six, twelve, and twenty-four months. Christmas time is a good time at the Digest. When the year's business justifies it—and it has justified it every year for 33 successive years—profits are split with Digest workers in a profit-sharing bonus. The amount that each worker will receive is announced at the end of the year; payment is made in January. Those who have been a year at the Digest share in full. Seasonal workers who have accumulated the equivalent of twelve months' service over the past five years also receive a full bonus.

The Digest provides at-work medical care. It pays two thirds of the premium for hospital and medical insurance. It pays 20 times what the worker contributes toward his liberal pension. It gives every worker a free copy of the Digest on publication of each issue and one free subscription on the employee's gift list at Christmas time. When they are issued, it charges employee purchasers just fifty cents for a volume of Reader's Digest Condensed Books, which retails at $2.44, and, three months after its publication, gives a copy to each worker. Digest employees can buy other magazines at a discount and obtain as much as 33⅓ per cent discount on all books they buy through the Digest. Employees may ask that music they prefer be played over the loud-speaker system, and special numbers for weddings and anniversaries are played on request. When a department plans a luncheon, tables are reserved for the party, the lunch-time schedule is changed to suit the revelers, and time is allowed to decorate the cafeteria tables. If Digest employees wish to go somewhere, the Digest's New York office handles their personal requests for air, rail, or ship travel.

It should be Utopia, but if it doesn't seem so you can say so. "Of course, there is still human nature as well as Nature out here," DeWitt Wallace and Lila Acheson Wallace tell new employees. "Please don't hesitate to speak up if there is anything that displeases or irritates you." If an employee has a problem or needs assistance he can talk it over with his department head, the personnel department, or "feel free to approach any executive of the Digest to ask for advice, air problems, or make suggestions."

Unless an employee is discharged for cause—which seldom or never happens—there is guaranteed severance pay of one week's pay after service of from six months to a year; up to six weeks' pay for those released after from four to five years of service, and two additional weeks' pay for every year of additional service up to an improbable limit of four months.

Leaves of absence can be arranged when it is necessary for personal reasons for an employee to have a longer period away from work than vacations provide. "One very nice type of leave of absence," says "You and The Reader's Digest" archly, "is a maternity leave. We request that you start your maternity leave not later than the sixth month of pregnancy. By then your heir is apparent!"

There are things that even The Reader's Digest cannot protect against. Social Security, federal income tax, and New York State Disability take their cuts out of the biweekly pay checks. The Digest itself takes only one. It fines employees for accumulated tardiness amounting to 15 minutes or more in any week and does not pay for absence from work except through illness. It asks employees not to make or receive personal telephone calls, except from pay stations provided, during business hours or to have personal mail addressed to them at work. These actions are indicative.

The Digest gives a lot. It expects at least a minimum return. The magazine expects, even demands, work cleanly, cheerfully, and accurately done, for the real business of the Digest is the Digest. It does not pretend to give something for nothing, a bargain arrangement universally admired but seldom of much advantage to either party. Its personnel department opens its discussion of the Digest and pension plan with an honest avowal: "We hope you'll stay here and enjoy working for the Digest the remainder of your working years. Since your services are valuable to us . . ."

The worker is expected to earn what he gets, but at the Digest he always gets a little more, or a little more than that—masterpieces of art to be looked at or ignored, lush furnishings in lounges and libraries, music that hath charms or can go unheard, a time to play if a time to work has been decently observed, privileges and perquisites of many kinds, and consideration not listed in any handbook.

It is scarcely to be wondered at, even though The Reader's Digest is only 36 years old, that 20 per cent of its employees have worked there for ten years or more, 3 per cent for twenty years or more, and a number have already been retired.

All the compensations cannot be described, but "You and The Reader's Digest" lists one more that makes the compilation of stated rewards either complete or, given its final touch, a little frightening. It can happen here but in few other places. "Each year the following service 'Oscars' are presented: to each woman on her tenth anniversary, a silver compact; to each man on his tenth anniversary, a gold pocketknife; to each Digester on his or her fifteenth anniversary, a silver desk-type traveling clock. Those who have completed 20 years at the Digest each receive two round-trip tickets to Bermuda, Puerto Rico, or elsewhere in the Caribbean and two extra weeks of vacation with pay to make the trip. These are but tokens of our heartfelt thanks for your long friendship and co-operation."

CHAPTER IX

CUTTING AND CONDENSING

The editorial process of selecting and preparing for publication in The Reader's Digest articles first published full-length in other periodicals is intense and painstaking. It is made up of search, judgment, selection, and condensation—of reading, screening, rereading, reappraisal, and re-editing by many people at every level of editorial authority up to DeWitt Wallace. The process is continuous from the time the piece is first spotted until, if it survives the ministrations of "murderer's row," it is set in type and scheduled for Digest publication.

Each month the Digest editorial staff spends more than 5000 hours in reading to find the articles for one issue. It has been estimated that one person would have to read steadily eight hours a day for 21 months to cover the same material.

Ten members of a designated reading and cutting staff, each responsible for examining 15 to 20 assigned magazines, weeklies or monthlies, regularly scrutinize 140 major English-language magazines and newspapers. Other Digest readers comb 450 additional periodicals, ranging from specialized scientific and educational journals and scholarly quarterlies through trade papers to company house organs. Editors in every Digest office abroad painstakingly cull foreign publications for possibilities.

Each member of the reading and cutting staff grades every article in the publications assigned him as "usable," "possible," or "not usable." He reaches these decisions by application of the same criteria DeWitt Wallace used when he worked single-handed in the New York Public Library in 1922. These are:

> *Is it quotable? Is it something the reader will remember, ponder and discuss?*
>
> *Is it applicable? Does it come within the framework of most people's interest and conversation? Does it touch the individual's own concerns?*
>
> *Is it of lasting interest? Will it still be of interest a year or two from now?*

As the reader grades, he cuts in the text of the original-publication articles selected as "usable" or "possible" to Digest length. He also writes down marginal comments: "This piece has some shock value"—"Lacks force"—"Material thin"—"Good ideas but badly expressed . . ." Reader selections, grades, cuts, and comments, all still on the original printed article in the original publication, go on to the editor who heads the reading and cutting staff.

This editor spot checks all articles marked "NU." He reads carefully all marked "U" or "P." He may disagree with the first reader and ask for another editorial opinion. He may hold a piece for further consideration. Those articles which sieve through his screening he sends on for consideration by the senior editor in charge of the issue of The Reader's Digest which is in preparation.

The editor in charge of the issue selects those of the articles which he believes will give color, variety, and balance to the magazine he is making up from condensed articles, Digest originals, and book condensations—the three chief ingredients of every issue of The Reader's Digest—and returns them for firm rather than tentative cutting.

The editor making the first cut, usually the editor who first spotted and approved the article in print, attempts to present its subject matter clearly and concisely in the words of its author. He deletes words, sentences, transitions, even paragraphs or whole sections which do not seem necessary to clear and complete exposition of the author's thoughts, cutting the article most often to about one-quarter its original length. Some articles are cut about one-half, some less. Not rules, but the nature of the subject and the author's treatment of it govern. The cutting varies with each article and what the Digest editors see in it and wish to highlight in their condensing. A briefly told story of importance may be republished in the Digest in nearly its original form—or the Digest may select only one section telling of some new development of general interest from a long technical article addressed primarily to specialists.

At this point the cutting process has only begun. After its first cut a typescript of the article is checked against the original by at least two more editors. It is retyped and returned to the editor in charge of the issue, who will examine it, perhaps cut further, perhaps restore some of the original. It goes from him to the managing editor, then to the executive editor, then probably to DeWitt Wallace, who for most of the years of the Digest's existence has seen and worked on every article appearing in the magazine. Any of these can, and usually does, make further editorial changes to shape the condensed article to Digest standards. The process is one of continued polishing through the attrition of many trained minds. Sometimes the attrition becomes erosion. The cutting and condensing wears away the too thin article, and it does not survive the operation.

While the Digest editors are cutting and condensing the article, trained researchers are checking it for its factual accuracy.

Articles which run the editorial and research gamut successfully are retyped to contain all the new cuts or restorations and sent on to the copy desk, where they are prepared for the printer. They go from the copy desk to the Digest's art department in New York City, where illustrations or graphic ornaments are prepared, from the art department to the printer in Dayton, where all Digests are now printed on the presses of the McCall Corporation, and the article is set in type. Page proofs—the Digest does not use galleys—return to Chappaqua on a 4-day schedule.

The cutting is still not over. The Digest's top editors may further condense or make additions to the article in proof. Just three editors make cuts on page proofs, where six or eight editors have cut and recut the original for the balance, emphasis, form, clarity, packed meaning that a Digest article must have. Often some of the author's first sentences or paragraphs are restored, and the finished product more closely resembles the original than did some of the intervening versions. The edited proofs are returned to Dayton for correction and resetting, and revised page proofs are sent back to the Digest. Cutting and editing continue right up to this point of no return, final editing being transmitted by telephone. Occasionally a scheduled article must be partly recast at this final stage through editor-to-composition room telephone calls that have been known to last up to two hours.

Where 190 pages of editorial material are needed for an issue, 220 to 240 may be prepared in final form through this editorial process so that last-minute changes, the dropping out of one article and the substitution of another, may be made where contingencies indicate. The addition of advertising to the Digest in 1955 made new demands for greater flexibility in the use of editorial space. There are never less than 180 editorial pages; usually there are more. Closing date for any issue is two months before publication. All material, both editorial and advertising, must be at the printer's in final form two months before the on-sale date of the issue in which it is to appear. The print run of The Reader's Digest is so enormous that it takes one full month of this time to put the issue through the press.

Cutting and condensing at The Reader's Digest has been called "a meeting of minds." It is the group editorial mind at work on sentence-by sentence, word-by-word scrutiny and consideration of every editorial piece, whether it has previously been published or is a Digest original. The imagination, critical skills, and even the literary quirks of one editor are worked against those of another until the article takes on finally a smoothness and appearance of effortless expression within the terms of the matter and manner of the original piece. Meaning is kept intact. The writer's style is carefully retained. Unless he makes textual comparison, it is often hard for the author himself to discover where passages have been deleted, words stricken, or sentences recast in the condensation of his work. Perhaps it takes this kind of group editing to prepare the tight, clear, easily understandable Digest article for its vast group audience.

The same editorial sifting and screening is applied to the titling. As each editor cuts and comments on an article, he also suggests possible titles. Digest titles, apt, pithy, colorful always, are selected from ten or twelve nominations or created out of suggestions provided by several.

The heart of Reader's Digest editing lies in this cutting and condensing. Only article selection is more important. This, in essence, is the editorial treatment which DeWitt Wallace devised and made a major element in the Digest's early success. It is done with meticulous care and done so expertly that it has attained almost the dimensions and characteristics of a minor art form which The Reader's Digest originated and has made peculiarly its own.

"I have yet to encounter an article that was seriously damaged by the condensation," decided H. L. Mencken, as severe a critic of American writing as the country has produced, "and I can recall dozens that were palpably improved."

CHAPTER X

EDITORIAL RESEARCH

Digest editors often complain that research has ruined many a good story. Sometimes after an article has been checked sensational disclosures emerge as somewhat less sensational. Sometimes what has been offered as true proves to be completely false. Few manuscripts survive unscathed the meticulous fact-by-fact checking of the Editorial Research Department in the Digest's New York offices.

Sixteen Digest researchers, young women who graduated at or near the top of their classes in Smith, Mt. Holyoke, Wellesley, Wells, Barnard, and other women's colleges, use every standard reference and whatever specialized sources are indicated by the nature of the article—selected and condensed or a Digest original —to verify the writer's statements. Every one of these is checked. Typically, some 2000 facts are traced through perhaps 450 sources in researching the contents of one issue of the Digest.

The Digest Editorial Research Department has its own reference collection of encyclopedias, almanacs, handbooks, foreign-language dictionaries, and shelves of volumes on medicine, sociology, psychology, and other subjects related to Digest content. It has *The New York Times Index* and the *Times* on microfilm, files of religious, political, and some foreign magazines and an extensive morgue of newspaper clippings filed under subject heads for ready reference. Thorough research on articles is done mostly at the nearby New York Public Library, one of the country's four or five complete research libraries. The researchers also use, as an article demands, the New York Society Library, the Engineering Society Library, the journalism morgue at the Columbia University School of Journalism, New York's Museum of Natural History, the Botanical Gardens, and other specialized collections. About half the editorial research of The Reader's Digest is done through library sources.

Digest researchers also interview authorities, consult the people with whom a writer has talked in gathering his facts, and endeavor to learn from discussion more facts than are available in published records alone.

Article manuscripts are returned to the Digest editors with every fact isolated, noted, underlined, and approved or disapproved. Typed sheets of a different color paper are interleaved among the manuscript pages. These carry notes on incorrect or questionable statements on the facing pages of the manuscript. Where a fact is designated incorrect, an explanation is given, the correct fact is supplied, and an alternate way of restating a passage so that it will be accurate is suggested. Appended to the whole is a list, numbered, of reference sources consulted. Every factual statement, correct or incorrect in the manuscript, carries the number of the source against which it has been checked.

A line in a recently checked article on the conversion of salt sea water to fresh water read in part ". . . and some islanders in the Persian Gulf and the Atlantic are drinking converted sea water . . ." Above this statement Research wrote, "See Note." The note on the page inset opposite read:

> *The islanders in the Persian Gulf (Bahrain) are not drinking sea water but brackish well water. The inhabitants of Kuwait, which borders on the Persian Gulf, do drink sea water (converted). Curacao and Aruba, whose inhabitants drink converted sea water, are in the Caribbean.*
>
> SUGGEST: ". . . *people living near the Persian Gulf, and some islanders in the Caribbean* . . ."
>
> SOURCES: 22,9

At another point the word "ocean" was objected to as being technically incorrect. The body of water mentioned was actually a "sea." It was suggested "salt water" be used. Sometimes when a correct substitution cannot reasonably be injected into the context of the article the suggestion reads merely "delete." This 11-page article necessitated reference to 33 different sources, publications, people, and institutions and resulted in 27 indicated revisions, most of them minor, a few extensive.

Occasionally an article under consideration or one in preparation by a Digest staff writer requires extensive leg work. A few years ago a Digest researcher, representing herself as a German student, attended classes at the Russian-controlled Humboldt University in order to compare instruction given there with that in the Free University in the western sector of Berlin. One envied Digest research worker drew the assignment of visiting seven European countries to find out whether a working girl could really enjoy a two weeks' holiday on the Continent for the sum travel agencies were advertising. Another tried out a new type diver's suit to find out whether it was as satisfactory as a writer claimed. Another trailed a Good Humor man to see whether his sales technique was what an article said it was. In London a researcher had to find out whether or not housemaids in Buckingham Palace were allowed to wear lipstick. She found no edict for or against.

All the work of Editorial Research does not result in the correction and revision of an article manuscript. Sometimes the fancifulness of the purported facts places it beyond saving. Several times a story too close for comfort to Digest publication has proved a complete fabrication.

Before Editorial Research was checking Digest book condensations, a World War II spy story that had no basis in fact actually got published. The Canadian veteran who claimed to have endured horrendous Nazi tortures and performed large feats of valor had already duped packed audiences from the platform, the professional journalist who had spent weeks with him taking detailed notes, and the New York book publisher who issued the full-length book.

A charming "Unforgettable Character" was purchased from an author in France. Told as a true-life experience of the author, the story described a gentle peasant shepherd in a mountainous region of Provence who, purely as a labor of love, planted a barren land with trees. The story was written with deft characterization and convincing detail. The author told of meeting Elzeard Bouffier, the shepherd, on a tramp before World War I, of visiting him after that war, and of going to see him again after World War II. He had walked with Bouffier through a forest of 10,000 oaks sprung from 20,000 acorns planted by the shepherd. Bouffier, he said, had also planted maples, birch, and linden. His labor of love had brought greenness to the earth, water where none had

This Van Gogh, one in The Reader's Digest Collection of Fine Arts, hangs in the reception room off the main lobby at Chappaqua. The Digest collection is composed of paintings of the French impressionist and modern schools. Monet, Manet, Braque, Redon, Modigliani and Degas are representative of the collection which hangs in the Digest offices and at High Winds.

The editorial headquarters of The Reader's Digest is notable both for its landscaping and its interior décor.

The esthetic attractiveness at The Reader's Digest reflects the taste and skill of Lila Acheson Wallace, who has directed the contouring and planting of the grounds and the decorating and furnishing of the buildings. The principal editorial offices are furnished with antiques; the others, with authentic reproductions in walnut and mahogany. Color has been used profusely to gain unusual effects of gaiety, light, and warmth.

WANN

The central rotunda at the main entrance to The Reader's Digest.

The reception room just off the rotunda lobby at Chappaqua.

A Chagall in
The Reader's Digest Collection.

A corner of DeWitt Wallace's spacious office at the Digest. The office has a formal fireplace flanked by deep leather chairs, pastel paneled walls. Chagall's "The Three Candles," pictured above, hangs here. The office exemplifies Mrs. Wallace's intent and achievement of having Digest editorial offices resemble studies in well-appointed private homes.

FORBERT

The editorial library at The Reader's Digest is paneled in distinctively carved rare butternut. It provides standard references for the use of all Digest editors. More extensive and detailed reference sources are in the Research Department of The Reader's Digest in New York, where all Digest articles are carefully checked for accuracy before publication in the magazine.

Looking from a Digest hall through the library outdoors to some of the lawns and gardens.

A famous Renoir in
The Reader's Digest Collection.

The office of Lila Acheson Wallace at The Reader's Digest. The harmonious use of bright and subdued colorings enhances the effects gained through its delicate appointments. Its grace contrasts with the more formal dignity of the library and some of the other offices.

WANN

WANN

There are some
employee lounge
The Reader's Dig
Each has its o
special decor. E
is furnished w
good reproducti
of fine originals,
plicates of wh
employees, if t
wish, can purch
for use in furnish
their own homes

The feminine air of the garden lounge, above, contrasts with the masculine appearance of the Men's Firehouse.

WANN

Office of Kenneth W. Payne, Executive Editor, The Reader's Digest.

Office of A. L. Cole, General Business Manager, The Reader's Digest.

A Matisse in
The Reader's Digest Collection

Office of Ralph E. Henderson, Editor, Reader's Digest Condensed Books.

BARNELL

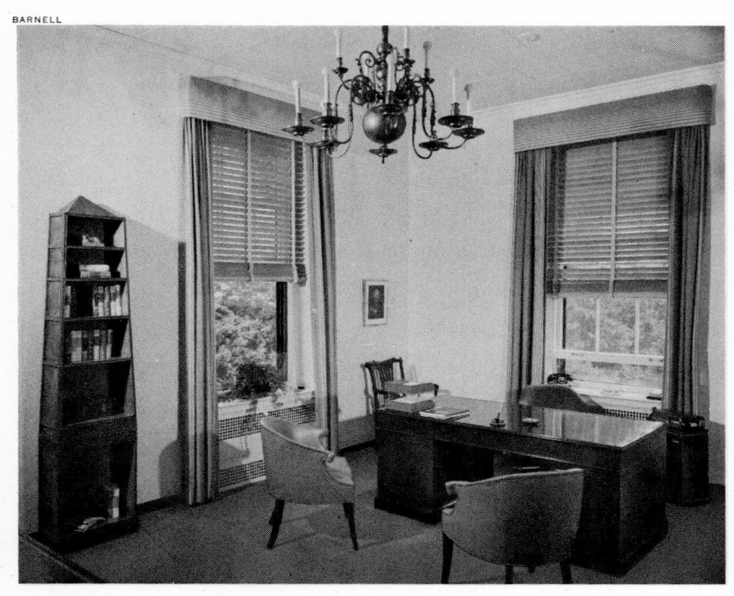

Office of Paul W. Thompson, General Manager, International Editions.

flowed before, and happiness to the once miserable village of Vergons. It was a delightful tale.

A Digest research worker from the Paris office started out on a routine check. She talked with prefects, mayors, foresters, tradespeople, and the ancients of Vergons and a dozen Alpine hamlets near by. She inspected the land where the author showed her on a map that Bouffier had planted his forests. She checked church and village records. What she finally discovered was that no Elzeard Bouffier had ever been born in that region. He had kept no sheep. He had planted no trees. As far as the records and the memories of Père Marius, the 80-year-old forest ranger of Saint-Étienne-Les-Orgues, the 90-year-old former Judge Paul Jaubert of Banon, or the 75-year-old Marcellin Poisson of Contadour showed, he had never lived. He had never so much as died.

One of the armed forces sent out publicity releases on an enlisted man in its medical branch who, by dint of energy and application, had managed to complete medical school while still on active duty in many different places. It was a good story. One of the medical journals picked it up and printed it. A roving editor was assigned to build it into a Digest piece. The writer interviewed the man and got his story, talked with his commanding officers and with public-relations officers. The story checked with the records. Its hero on duty, dispensing medicines and giving psychological tests, was articulate and plausible.

When Editorial Research started to check, they found no record of the man's attendance at some of the medical schools he had listed. As he had stated that he had been in some of them for only a short time and as some of the schools' records were incomplete, minor discrepancies did not arouse immediate suspicion. Two schools, proud of the man's achievement, after reading the account in the medical journal, assumed he had been their student. Then someone noticed that the story subject claimed a master's degree from a European university which, at that time, did not grant an M.A. Service records were rechecked, officers reinterviewed, the medical schools requestioned. The man, by this time on foreign duty, was not immediately available. On his return he was ordered to Washington where, under long and hard questioning, he finally admitted that his entire story was untrue.

Digest Research performs still another function, one of importance on any publication. Besides checking with library sources and authorities in their special fields of interest, Digest researchers check with the legal advisers to the magazine on any matter which is potentially libelous, could be construed as an invasion of privacy, or in any other way constitute recognizable offense. Because the most innocent-appearing material can sometimes be used as cause for complaint, this legal advice is sought and used in order to provide whatever documentation is necessary for a given statement, learn what releases must be obtained before publication, and know what suggestions need to be made for the rewording or deletion of suspect passages.

CHAPTER XI

EDITORS AND ROVING EDITORS

In the early and middle 1930s, as The Reader's Digest underwent swift transformation from a purely eclectic little magazine to a large-circulation magazine with its own force and distinctness, DeWitt Wallace gathered about him the skilled professionals who have become the Digest's top editors and writers.

Many of them had been editors of the literary and intellectual magazines from which Wallace condensed material during the Digest's formative years. Kenneth W. Payne, executive editor of the Digest, who was educated at the University of Wisconsin and the Sorbonne, had been in turn editor of *Popular Science Monthly, People's Home Journal,* managing editor of *McClure's,* then editorial director of the proud *North American Review.* Alfred S. Dashiell, the Digest's managing editor, had been managing editor of the *Daily Princetonian* during his undergraduate years. He worked briefly as a reporter on the *Baltimore Evening Sun,* then in 1924 joined *Scribner's* as an assistant editor, becoming managing editor of that magazine in 1930. Senior Editor Paul Palmer, Harvard educated, had been a reporter and Sunday editor on the St. Louis *Post-Dispatch,* then Sunday editor of the New

York *World*. Later he was editor and publisher of the *American Mercury*. Senior Editor Marc Rose had helped found *Business Week,* then become its editor. Merle Crowell had been editor of the *American Magazine;* Fulton Oursler, of *Liberty*.

During this same period DeWitt Wallace hired as members of the Digest's staff writers who worked on Digest assignments. Charles W. Ferguson, a graduate of Southern Methodist, was a circuit rider in Texas when H. L. Mencken spotted his writing in the *Southwest Review* and asked him to write for the *American Mercury*. He came to New York, became religious editor for George H. Doran, and was both writing for *Harper's* and serving as president of the Round Table Press when DeWitt Wallace approached him to write for the Digest. Ferguson, one of the first writers to sign an original article in the Digest, became a staff member in 1934. He is now a senior editor. Ferguson's *Naked to Mine Enemies,* a notable biography of Cardinal Wolsey, was published in 1958. Henry Morton Robinson, a Roman Catholic writer best known now for his novel, *The Cardinal,* was an instructor in English at Columbia and past editor of *Contemporary Verse* when he joined the Digest as an associate editor in 1935.

Wallace hired other writers for article production, then in 1940 conceived the idea of the roving editor. The roving editors listed on the masthead of The Reader's Digest are not editors at all but writers whose names appear frequently on signed articles in the magazine. They are the permanent writing staff of the Digest living in various parts of the country and the world who write exclusively for The Reader's Digest. It was DeWitt Wallace's idea that "given the security of a monthly stipend, most writers would do a better job. They would have the financial means to take the time to go scouting for article ideas, to explore the possibilities of an article, and to make sure that what they wrote was the last word, as of that time, on that particular subject."

There are 16 such roving editors now listed on the Digest's masthead. The names of the first three appeared in May 1940: Barclay Acheson, late Chairman of International Editions; Karl Detzer; and Paul Palmer. In June 1941 came Stanley High, a Methodist minister who had become a foreign correspondent for *The Christian Science Monitor,* then editor of the *Christian Herald.* Max Eastman, editor of Karl Marx, translator of Pushkin and Trotsky, a communist who while editor of *The Masses* was twice tried for sedition, was also made a roving editor in 1941. Eastman, who broke with Stalinism in the 1920s, was both an authority on communism and the author of a minor critical classic, *The Enjoyment of Poetry,* 1913, and a companion study, *The Enjoyment of Laughter,* 1936.

William Hard, an instructor in history at Northwestern who became a political writer for *The Nation,* the *New Republic,* and the newspaper wire service, was added in June 1942. In November 1942 six more roving editors were appointed, the best known, the wit, raconteur—whimsical and waspish member of the Algonquin literati who helped found *The New Yorker*—Alexander Woollcott. Woollcott, whom DeWitt Wallace has described as "the most enthusiastic and productive roving editor of them all," died within the year, but in five months he wrote six Digest pieces, among them his last, a story of Supreme Court Justice Oliver Wendell Holmes, which Woollcott proudly called one of the best he had ever written.

Fulton Oursler, author of *The Greatest Story Ever Told, The Greatest Faith Ever Known,* and other best-selling religious books, joined the staff in 1944. Although listed as a senior editor, he was from then until his death in 1952 a prolific writer of religious and inspirational articles for the Digest, one of the magazine's best-known and most characteristic writers during that period.

The Digest's editors and writers—roving editors and others who, while not listed on the masthead, are paid a retainer to give the Digest first call on their production—represent a wide variety of backgrounds, viewpoints, and interests. Most of the roving editors work within special fields. William Hard is responsible for many of the articles on public affairs. Lester Velie specializes in labor problems, Francis Vivian Drake in aviation, Stanley High in evangelical religion, Harland Manchester in science. Donald Culross Peattie, a botanist with the U. S. Department of Agriculture early in his career, later a newspaper columnist and writer of nature books, does the Digest's familiar imaginative articles on nature. William L. White, son of the famous Emporia, Kansas, newspaper editor, has written best-selling books on Digest assignment: *Queens Die Proudly, London Fire, Journey for Margaret,* all of which appeared as Reader's Digest book condensations. James Michener, author of *South Pacific,* wrote both *The Bridge at Andau,* which appeared as a book condensation in March 1957, and *While Others Sleep,* the story of the Strategic Air Command, condensed October 1957, on Digest assignment.

A huge, robustious Michigander of Dutch extraction, Paul de Kruif is undoubtedly the most controversial of the roving editors. De Kruif, who first taught bacteriology at the University of Michigan, where he received his doctorate, was on the research staff of the Rockefeller Institute in 1920 when Glenn Frank asked him to write a series of medical articles for the *Century.* "With brilliant sarcasm," wrote Ben Hibbs, since 1942 editor of *The*

Saturday Evening Post, but when he wrote in 1938 an editor of *Country Gentleman,* for which De Kruif was then writing, "he took the pants off the medical profession."

The irreverence and iconoclasm were so marked in the anonymous articles, which as *Our Medicine Men,* 1922, became De Kruif's first book, that he was fired. Ambitious then to become a satirical novelist, De Kruif joined Sinclair Lewis as a collaborator on *Arrowsmith,* 1925. Martin Arrowsmith in the novel was patterned partly after De Kruif. His own best seller, *Microbe Hunters,* was published in 1926, and Paul de Kruif was established not as a novelist but as a colorful reporter of the epics of medical science and a vigorous translator of medical material into lay language.

One of the most prolific of the roving editors, De Kruif has been warmly lauded and sometimes severely censured by organized medicine for some of his many Digest articles on new medical discoveries, new drugs, new cures, new diseases, and on the medical profession. The complaints have declined as his crusading articles have reached a wider and wider public. In recent years most of his Digest articles have first been published in *Today's Health,* published by the American Medical Association, and the A.M.A. has suggested few changes in either subject matter or approach. Meanwhile De Kruif's credits have mounted with publication of many books since his famous *Microbe Hunters.* Among them have been: *Hunger Fighters, Men Against Death, Life Among the Doctors, The Fight for Life,* and *A Man Against Insanity.*

The other roving editors usually write within their own fields of interest. Lois Mattox Miller, formerly an editor and columnist with women's magazines, does health and medical articles. Karl Detzer, until recently himself a newspaper publisher in Michigan, does articles on business and community affairs. The late J. P. McEvoy, a familiar Digest by-line, wrote everything from greeting-card verse to short stories and novels and three editions of the Ziegfeld Follies. His field was entertainment. Robert Littell, who had been a newspaper drama critic, does literary, historical, and political pieces. Roving editors who live in London and Paris actually function as European correspondents for the Digest. With Max Eastman less active, Russian-born Eugene Lyons, who spent 6 years in the Soviet as a United Press Correspondent before becoming in turn editor of the *American Mercury* and *Pageant,* is the Digest's principal writer on communism. He is the author of *Assignment in Utopia, Moscow Carousel,* and other books on Russian subjects.

Roughly what DeWitt Wallace did in devising the roving-editor concept was build up a stable of writers for the Digest much as S. S. McClure built up his staff of reform journalists for *McClure's* and as George Horace Lorimer did at *The Saturday Evening Post* when he developed writers of fiction like Kenneth Roberts, J. P. Marquand, Mary Roberts Rinehart, and a dozen others.

Most of the roving editors were established writers or competent journalists before appointment to the Digest staff. Like the Digest's leading editors, they are professionals from divergent backgrounds whose varied experience and special interests combine to afford the magazine the wide coverage of subjects of broad human appeal which the Digest brings its readers. Their talents vary in kind and degree. Some are primarily research men who can dig out the facts and marshal them in order for analysis and understanding. Others are primarily rewrite men, writers who can present the facts clearly and imaginatively. Some are reporters in the investigative newspaper tradition. At Digest instigation or pursuing ideas of their own approved by the Digest editors, the roving editors travel widely in the United States and abroad in search of material.

Roving editors act almost as independent agents, covering their fields for stories, continually seeking story ideas, and, after checking with Chappaqua, following through on them. Occasionally a roving editor will travel half the country to track down a story, then discard it after investigation because it proves untrue or turns out to be what is obviously not Digest material. The acceptance rate of articles from the roving editors is high, though sometimes an article or even a book-length piece will be rejected by the editors, even after they have initially approved the idea, as not meeting the current needs of the magazine.

The reverse can happen. The editors have rejected a rover's story idea, then changed their minds and accepted the finished piece after the roving editor has gone ahead with a subject which interested him and written the story anyway. The roving editors of The Reader's Digest do their own leg work, supplying and checking their own facts. Digest Research not only checks these facts, but also often provides additional information for the writer's use. Roving editors write their stories in full, submitting articles that run usually from 20 to 50 typed pages. They do not attempt to edit or condense. As with writing from all other sources, the editing and condensing is done at Chappaqua. It is Digest editorial belief that a subject must be fully encompassed before it can be satisfactorily condensed.

The stories behind some of the stories produced by the Digest's roving editors are often as colorful as the published stories themselves. A roving editor dutifully attending an international labor conference in Geneva found the proceedings dull. He sought out the UN executive whose agency was running the meetings.

"Any interesting reports lately?"

"One of our staff men may be writing one. He's just back from behind the Iron Curtain."

The UN staff man proved to be an English engineer. "Queer chaps, those Yugoslavs," he told the roving editor. "They're tinkering like mad with communism."

"You mean they're downgrading Marx?" asked the rover excitedly. "Where do I go? Whom do I see?"

The engineer told him. The roving editor grabbed an English-speaking Yugoslav delegate to the conference, who helped him get a visa, then caught the next plane to Belgrade. Inside Yugoslavia twelve hours later, friendly Yugoslavs worked an 18-hour day with the roving editor, answering all his questions, showing him all he asked to see. The Yugoslavs had turned back most expropriated farm land to private peasant owners. They were experimenting with local management of factories. Back in Switzerland 3 weeks later, the roving editor found time to report to the Digest's managing editor and ask approval of his story. The editor's reply did not catch up with him until he had returned to the United States and written his article.

The piece which appeared in The Reader's Digest in 1956 was the first intimation of restiveness in the Russian satellites and of the disenchantment of some satellite leaders with communist dogma. It was published almost simultaneously with the workers' uprising in Poland, giving Digest readers some notion of what the explosion was about.

Like any reporter, the roving editor must often dig his story out of files, compilations of statistics, government reports, interviews, painfully piling up and checking facts. He may base his story on laboratory reports or on the recitals of inarticulate and sometimes reluctant witnesses, piecing bits together, verifying the whole after he had got his facts and interpretation. Sometimes a lead works out excitingly to an exclusive or a story which can break in the Digest before other sources have discovered the facts.

The Digest published an enlightening article on James R. Hoffa 2 years before the Senate Rackets Committee placed him on the front pages of the newspapers. The Digest's roving editor who specializes in labor articles was crisscrossing the country getting at first hand stories of union men who were being pushed around by their leaders. He noticed that time and time again when underworld figures wanted favors inside labor they reached out for a Teamster vice-president in Chicago. This ninth vice-president, then virtually unknown to the public, was James Hoffa.

The roving editor flew out to Chicago and spent two afternoons talking with Hoffa. The Teamster boss talked so freely and with such seeming candor that the rover was shaken in his conviction that Hoffa was a rising power with sinister connections, but he did notice that a Hoffa bodyguard and errand boy was entrusted with millions of dollars of Teamster welfare-insurance-fund money.

"How can a onetime hood here in Chicago get rich Teamster insurance business without having to split with the Capone boys?" he asked an underworld informant.

"He can't," was the answer.

The roving editor made flying trips to union locals dominated by Hoffa. He found that union members were deprived of meetings and elections. He uncovered other evidences that verified his earlier suspicions. The Reader's Digest published his article. Two years later Hoffa was excoriated by both the Senate Rackets Committee and the AFL-CIO Ethical Practices Committee.

All Digest roving editors do not indulge in such Richard Harding Davis exploits, but some of those whose ideas and assignments call for this kind of investigative work do enough of it so that they are sometimes asked whether their work is not dangerous. Have they ever been threatened?

One roving editor likes to tell this story in reply. The head of a union local in Chicago whom he had described as a gangster in a Digest article wrote asking him to see him when he was next in the city. The roving editor called on the man in his office in a rebuilt motion-picture house on the West Side. The union officer asked what "gangster" actually meant, and the two men amicably discussed the term, the Chicagoan's gang associations, and his criminal record. When they had finished, the local union head suggested that the roving editor might like to look around the hall. The recreation quarters and bar in the basement were worth seeing.

Followed by a third man who kept his hands in his coat pockets, they headed for a dark flight of stairs into the basement. As the roving editor groped for the handrail, the union head grasped his arm.

"Hey, wait!" he pleaded. "Don't move until I turn on the light. All I need is you should fall and hurt yourself."

The roving editors do not have offices at Digest headquarters, but they are frequently in Chappaqua discussing story ideas with the editors or at the other end of a telephone. Sometimes they change places. Roving editors become senior editors or senior editors become roving editors, or a writer whose articles are prominent in the magazine works on a retainer without designated portfolio. Sometimes the change in title means change in assignment; sometimes it does not. DeWitt Wallace tries to keep his line-up flexible for adjustment to changing situations, meshing duties and abilities as the needs of The Reader's Digest dictate.

CHAPTER XII

THE EDITORIAL PROCESS

Editorial communication at The Reader's Digest is carried on largely through osmosis and contagion. There are no stated staff meetings or scheduled planning sessions. There are few channels, and these are not direct. There is no taut chain of command. Except in the cutting and condensing process, there are few fixed editorial routines.

An article idea may originate with DeWitt Wallace, with the executive editor, with the managing editor, or any one of the senior editors. A staff editor may propose it to a roving editor or an outside writer, or a roving editor may suggest it to Wallace or one of the other editors in authority at the Digest. An author or a literary agent may approach the Digest with an article or an article idea at an informal luncheon. There are many of these luncheons with two or three editors, a writer, an agent, or both, perhaps DeWitt Wallace, discussing possibilities, accepting this, rejecting that. Decisions are made or as often avoided while a fruitful idea is left to germinate or a barren one to perish. Some roving editors or writers on assignment report directly to DeWitt Wallace, others to another of the top echelon editors. Editors wander in and out of each other's offices, with or without a manuscript or a sheaf of notes as symbol that the visit is legitimate Digest business.

Most Digest editors find it difficult to explain how The Reader's Digest is put together, how they know and why they are certain that a piece printed in some other periodical should be chosen for the Digest, where and how original material originates. They cannot outline the exact physical procedure, much less describe the fusion of thought, emotion, experience, journalistic acumen, and editorial judgment that produces each issue of The Reader's Digest. They do not know, or do not know consciously. The question disturbs, just as it disturbs a man to be asked why he puts his left shoe or his right shoe on first and exactly how he does it.

The cadre of top Digest editors and writers came together when the magazine was comparatively small, worked together intensely and informally in a simple structure. Despite the growth of the magazine to world-wide proportions, that simplicity still obtains. The Digest has grown in size but not, editorially, in operating complexity. These men came to the Digest because they were attracted to and convinced by the Digest idea. They share or reflect the beliefs, ideas, and feelings of DeWitt Wallace. They like the kind of articles he likes, know how to recognize them and how to develop and produce them.

From the beginning DeWitt Wallace sought out what to him were "articles of lasting interest." The search was for timeless articles of universal human appeal. To find this in many fields of interest to the general reader and to insure a wide variety of subject matter in each issue of The Reader's Digest he devised a list of more than 25 categories which he tried consistently to cover. Classifications overlapped in the magazine as the subjects do in actuality. There has seldom been an article on each subject in every issue. The pattern was not made into a formal statement of contents, nor was it rigidly applied, but Wallace used it for years in shaping up succeeding issues of the Digest.

Roughly these categories were:

Adventure and Exploration
Agriculture—Conservation
Art of Living
Automobiles—Traffic Problems
Aviation
Biographies—usually several in each issue, most of them of well-known people but, as "Unforgettable Characters," often of obscure men and women
Business
Civic Affairs—Community Betterment
Communism
Crime and Punishment—Detection, Court Trials
Economics
Education—Child Raising
Entertainment—Movies, Sports, Radio, and later Television
Fine Arts
First-Person Stories—Autobiography
Government and Politics
Health
History—Historical Vignettes
Humor
Industry—Industrial Relations, Labor
International Relations

Literature and Journalism
Medical Science
Military Affairs—Problems of Defense
Natural Science—Nature and Animals
Rackets
Religion
Sex—Marriage, Divorce, Human Relations
Travel

These are the elements which compose the Digest story. The Digest's editors and their staff make this story read so simply that there is no pain in the act of reading, generally pleasure in what is read. The twentieth-century reader, besieged and enfevered by the mounting confusions of the increasingly complex world in which he lives, can see a little more clearly, and he is reassured.

By definition—it is a cliché of the periodical-publishing industry—the purpose of the magazine, any magazine of repute, is to inform and to entertain. The Digest has added one more aim. It states its purpose differently, means it, and practices it. The stated purpose of The Reader's Digest as phrased by Managing Editor Alfred S. Dashiell is "to inform, inspire, and entertain." The editors strive to do all three.

In achieving the total effect planned, manner of treatment is as important as matter treated. The Digest simplifies much of life into terms that men and women can understand and want to believe. The Digest is both stimulant and anodyne. By keeping its content as far as possible in simple, human terms, the Digest makes contemporaneity seem understandable against a background of history seen in the same terms. That this is deliberate editorial attempt seems doubtful, but the effect is achieved. The Digest often presents a better, simpler, happier world than, in the experience of most, exists outside its pages.

The Digest editors speak often of "balance." By it they mean a balance of the wide variety of material in each issue but also a balance weighted by the triple factors of information, inspiration, and entertainment. Usually there is a balance of humor, articles on personalities, articles on health and medical subjects, and articles on the art of living. It is, of course, not as bare as all that. There is no fixed editorial formula at the Digest. It seldom observes even its own flexible restrictions. It would be more accurate to say that there is always humor in the Digest, earthy humor some of it, humor touched with sentiment; that there are always parables of unforgettable characters; that there is usually a hard-hitting investigation into some phase of current affairs; that there is usually a stirring adventure narrative; that there is often a journalistic medical article; that there is always a piece on the art of thinking or feeling or managing a wife or husband or outwitting a baby or reading or giving or receiving a compliment—or just the art of living that includes them all.

Digest editors seek to find or fashion pieces that have "applicability." By this they mean articles that are applicable to the average reader in his daily life, subjects that reach out and touch him where he lives by himself among his fellows, articles that strike through clearly and warmly to the quick of his existence. The humor, personality, health, and art-of-living pieces all have this applicability. There are other subjects that have it.

People do not like to be ordered about. They do not like to be defrauded. Neither do Digest editors. They do not like the abuses of power by big government, big labor, big advertisers—

or the violation of trust by garage mechanics or electronics repairmen or anyone else. With the crusading zeal that is often a concomitant of idealism, they say so in blunt Digest pieces. Without pretense to the sophistication which finds it suspect, they believe in goodness, and they say that too. They believe in the heroism of ordinary men and women, in the ability of man to rise above adverse circumstances, and they show him doing it.

At the same time, for editorial canniness too is fused with idealism at the Digest, they know what Digest readers like and approve, the kind of material they expect to find in the magazine and read with greatest relish.

Sex is a part of life. It is of consuming interest to most people. It has never agreed to go away if ignored. The Digest does not neglect it, either in articles about the social and biological relationships of men and women or in its prose-poetic accounts of animal life in nature. Nostalgia is a human weakness. Its sweet sadness is somewhere in most issues of the Digest. Indignation assails most people. On occasion the Digest can be as indignant, and as incautious in its indignation, as the average man.

People thrill to tales of true adventure. They always have. It is to be hoped they always will. The narrative elements of adventure, often of mystery and suspense, are clear in many of the condensed-book supplements and often in the articles, for many Digest articles have a strong story base. Digest editors try, as they phrase it, "to make an article march." The narrative article marches more surely than the static discussion.

All of these are approximations merely tangential to the point of central creativeness in The Reader's Digest's editorial actuality and performance. That point lies deep in the instinct, the genius, the intuition, the perception, the compulsion—it has been called all of these and more—of DeWitt Wallace. This is the magic touchstone at the Digest, the elusive and mysterious force governing its total effort and inciting its unmatched success. Whatever it is, it is inexplicable except in terms of Wallace's character, temperament, and talent. If it is inexplicable, it is also real. It exists at Chappaqua, and it works surely.

Again, and understandably, Digest editors are helpless to explain. One of them attempting to sum up an attempt could say only, "If Wally likes it, automatically twelve million other people will like it. It's like that." This is answer enough as far as it goes, but there is a point at which DeWitt Wallace must translate unconscious understanding through identity with mass taste, if it is that, into conscious editorial judgment, make a decision, and act on it. This takes courage and skill as well as intuitive understanding of words in patterns and people in a few million more. Wallace has demonstrated both ever since his initial gamble against ridiculous odds in 1922. Perhaps all of these qualities are necessary to a man who—with the accomplishments of The Reader's Digest as fairly conclusive evidence—must rank as one of the great editors of the twentieth century.

CHAPTER XIII

HUMOROUS FILLER

Most periodicals, newspapers or magazines, use fillers, short items inserted at the ends of articles which do not complete the page or in other spots left blank by the exigencies of make-up. Generally, they are dull enough—a count of the number of sheep in Australia, the craters of the moon, or the hairs in a gross of heads, any informative item with the right number of lines and characters to fill the space. The Reader's Digest has made its fillers bright, amusing, varied, as much a part of the packed little magazine as its condensed articles, books, and other standard editorial features. Though the feature has been widely imitated, Digest fillers are a trade-mark of the magazine.

There were fillers in the first issue of The Reader's Digest, two of them. One was a half-page extract from a piece by Heywood Broun in *Judge*. Titled "Hart of the World," a typical Digest pun, it told of the influence of the movies on human behavior. The Hart, of course, was William S. The other filler, "Sid Says," was not amusing, nor was it meant to be. An extract from an editorial in the *American Magazine,* it described by implication a serious purpose of the new periodical: ". . . the most remarkable men in the world are eternal collectors of facts."

For some years there were no more fillers in The Reader's Digest. Every odd space was put to use for subscription appeals and teaser blurbs for articles to come in the issue for the following month. In July 1930 came a collection of amusing epitaphs culled from graveyard stones. In August came filler excerpts from *The Christian Science Monitor*. They dealt with the niceties of personal dispute in China.

> *The Chinese present an invaluable social contribution in the conception of getting along with one another. The citizenry have always been taught the virtue of self-restraint. . . .*
>
> *When a quarrel arises, disputants may shout noisily at each other, but each has the assurance that the other will not punch his face. Then, when both have given vent to their emotions, they manage to compromise. The way street quarrels usually end is for some third individual standing in the crowd to step forward and mediate.*
>
> *An old proverb reads: By fighting you never get enough, by yielding you get more than you expected. Laotzu said, "By bending we survive."*

Since January 1933 fillers have appeared regularly in the Digest. They come from everywhere. They come from life, books, magazines, newspapers, and they come in bulk. They come via the excerpt staff of the Digest, which reads only for filler material, from other Digest editors, from readers—and some of them come again and again and again.

All members of the Digest's magazine-reading staff watch for fillers. Often an article which is not suitable for Digest condensation may yield an anecdote or a single sentence to serve as a striking, one-line filler. From 1929 until the operation was discontinued in 1953 the group of researchers stationed at the Cleveland Public Library was a primary source of filler material. Professional readers searching for books to be condensed for the magazine or The Reader's Digest Book Club note possible fillers. The excerpt staff itself checks 600 magazines and house organs for fillers and covers newspapers from all parts of the country. Digest staff members are on the alert for fillers when they read for pleasure, when they listen to the radio or watch television, go to the movies or a play. Some Digest fillers have been overheard at parties or picked up from casual conversation.

The search for Digest fillers continues even abroad. London, Montreal, Copenhagen, and Paris staff members send them in. This one, used in the Digest not long ago, came in translated from the Paris office:

> *As a young Frenchman pushed his son's carriage down the street, the youngster howled with rage. "Please, Bernard, control yourself," the father said quietly. "Easy there, Bernard, keep calm!"*
>
> *"Congratulations, monsieur," said a woman who had been watching. "You know just how to speak to infants—calmly and gently." Then, leaning over the carriage, she said, "So the little fellow's named Bernard?"*
>
> *"No, madame," corrected the father. "He's named André.* I'm *Bernard."*
>
> —JEAN PIERRE VAILLARD *in* L'Anneau d'Or

As soon as it was published in the Digest, this anecdote began to appear in Americanized versions in American magazines and newspapers, flattery of imitation to which the Digest has long been accustomed. The newer versions were promptly submitted to the Digest by scores of readers.

Digest readers are one of the most fruitful, as well as one of the most industrious, sources of fillers. In addition to the items they send to the regular Digest departments such as "Life in These United States," "Life in This Wide World," "Humor in Uniform," and "Personal Glimpses," readers submit thousands of filler items each month. Some readers are so indefatigable in covering their local newspapers that the Digest staff has ceased to read them, considering those possible sources thoroughly covered. Some of the most successful contributors of Digest fillers are prisoners. Men in the Ohio State Penitentiary have sometimes averaged an acceptance a month, a high average, since contributors are paid only for being the first to spot an item.

One Ohio State Penitentiary inmate, in for passing bad checks, was a star contributor. His output was limited when, paroled, he was immediately jailed by Pennsylvania where there were no typewriters, outgoing letters were limited, and newspapers were scarce. His Digest filler career was ended by the stringent regulations at his next stop, the federal prison at Ashland, Kentucky.

A one-year-old Cadillac was offered for sale in a Long Island newspaper for $50. People thought it a joke, but, when the advertisement appeared for the third day, one imaginative man decided to investigate. He drove to the address given, a magnificent estate. An attractive middle-aged woman acknowledged the advertisement, showed him the car, which was in perfect condition. After driving it, he could not pay her the $50 fast enough to close the deal. With the bill of sale safe in his pocket, he dared ask why the woman sold for $50 a car which commanded a price of several thousand dollars.

"My late husband's will," she demurely explained, "left instructions that proceeds from the sale of his Cadillac were to go to his secretary who had been so kind to him."

Humor being what it is and people what they are, this story had started in California with the car a Chevrolet, reached New York with the car a Cadillac, and appeared in Winchell's column with a Long Island setting. The anecdote reappeared regularly in the Digest mail for months.

In February 1954 the Associated Press sent out a wire story on a Providence man whose car battery had gone dead on the Merritt Parkway. A woman driver volunteered to push him into a start, though he explained that, as his car had an automatic transmission, she would have to get up to 30 to 35 miles an hour. The woman nodded wisely. The man climbed behind his wheel and waited for her to line her car up behind his. She was so long about it that he turned to find out where she was. She was there—about 30 feet back and coming at him squarely at 35 miles an hour. Damage to his car was $300.

The story had been printed as fact by the Providence *Bulletin*, deluded by a prankster who had read it as a joke in a Boston paper. The Digest had already received more than 100 accounts of the "true" story even before the AP put it on the wire. The same story came in from Massachusetts, California, Texas, Illinois, Michigan, Pennsylvania, Connecticut—even from the Panama Canal Zone, where the road was not the Merritt Parkway but the Trans-Isthmian Highway. In each case the writer claimed to be the mother, close friend, fiancée, neighbor, garage repairman, automobile-insurance agent, or whatnot of the man driver. No one seemed to want to claim relationship with the woman. Anyway, according to one version of the story in which she was a wife pushing her husband, she was hospitalized with a fractured skull. That is probably the reason she never sent in the story herself. Everybody else did.

A major problem of the Digest's filler editors is keeping track of what stories have and have not been used before. They maintain an elaborate index, but humor is not made for the purposes of humorless systems of classification. Inevitably, for as professional humorists have pointed out, there are only so many good stories possible, some fillers are repeated. Not long ago a high-school teacher submitted two anecdotes she thought, so she wrote, would be ideal. They were, but they were almost word for word from back issues of The Reader's Digest. One of the excerpt editors was taken aback not long ago when her fourteen-year-old son triumphantly informed her that a filler in the current issue had been used in 1938. He had been amusing himself reading copies published before he was born.

When a slip-up does occur there seem to be innumerable faithful readers who have just been reading back issues of The Reader's Digest, spot the repetition, and delightedly write in to tell the editors of their discovery. Certain chestnuts appear with regularity in the mail. Often a reader relishing a filler anecdote in the current Digest repeats it to a friend, who repeats it to a friend, who repeats it to a friend or enemy until, promptly, it is resubmitted to The Reader's Digest quite innocently by an ambitious contributor, who has heard it told with no indication of its published source.

"A woman is as old as she looks. A man is old when he stops looking." The page of "Remarkable Remarks" in the first issue of

The Reader's Digest in 1922 attributed this quip to Rev. C. B. Preston. How many times this bit of wisdom—attributed to everybody from Benjamin Franklin or Mark Twain to the inventiveness of the contributor himself—has been resubmitted, the editors have long since lost count.

What is more surprising is that the quality of the original stories from reader contributors is amazingly high. Some of the freshest Digest filler material is obtained from them and often published with little or no editing needed. The fillers and regular departments of humor in the Digest are often what a reader first turns to on opening a new issue. They constitute what many of them think of as The Reader's Digest in its happiest mood. They entertain, stimulate the reader to submit what has amused him when he heard, saw, or experienced it. In this way Digest fillers play an important part in creating reader response and in establishing the magazine as a two-way means of mass communication.

CHAPTER XIV

"LIFE IN THESE UNITED STATES"

"Life in These United States" is always one of the brightest spots in The Reader's Digest. This is not professionally concocted work with every effect skillfully contrived. It is, unpolished, unguarded, the very material of human nature. It is folk stuff, homely, everyday, kindly humor. These Digest pages reveal something of the temper and character of an entire people. They seem part, rather than mere expression, of a broad kinship underlying surface differences of race, religion, or politics.

Since it first appeared in April 1943, "Life in These United States" has been one of the most popular features in every issue of the Digest. It is a magnet which draws readers of every kind. The anecdotes are read, relished, repeated. The idiosyncrasies and eccentricities of Americans, anybody, anywhere—your neighbor or yourself—come to light here every month in 10 or 12 short tales of the comic or the somehow touching. That is part of it.

There is another part. The stories "must be true and unpublished, from your own experience, showing appealing or humorous side lights on the American scene." The Reader's Digest pays $100 for each contribution accepted, but there is a greater allure.

This is the reader's chance to be a writer. Here a man or woman can participate in the creation of the magazine. He can talk about himself and can tell someone besides his wife, husband, or neighbors of the funniest thing in the world that he just saw or heard or did. Like the reader-contributed filler bits, "Life in These United States" makes for the feeling of two-way magazine communication that is one of the secrets of the Digest's success. It offers the fascination of the gamble—many are sent but few are chosen—the satisfaction of publication, and the dual reward of money and applause.

The possibilities are many and seemingly irresistible. Every month The Reader's Digest receives more than 20,000 letters, each containing from one to a dozen anecdotes, submitted for "Life in These United States." By actual count, there had been 2,882,844 of these letters up to the fall of 1957. It is from about a quarter million annual submissions that the editors of the department select and recommend the roughly 150 anecdotes which are accepted and published every year. The rate of submission continues to increase. During the latest month for which figures are available 33,000 pieces were received.

Contributions to "Life in These United States" come from all parts of the country and many parts of the world. They come from all kinds of people—farmers and teachers, mechanics and housewives, corporation and college presidents, nuns and bishops, doctors, lawyers, merchants, chiefs. Contributions come in such volume that they are reshipped by the pound in laundry cases to ex-editors working part time in Cleveland, Tucson, Winston-Salem, Syracuse, Binghamton, and elsewhere, who help eight especially trained staff readers do the initial screening. Each story is read at least twice. Those which the first readers pick as outstanding go to the chief editor of the department, who makes recommendations to the top editors as to which of the 1000 to 1500 which pass the first readers each month shall be accepted and used. Successful contributors are notified, and payment is made on publication.

Some stories which do not quite qualify for "Life in These United States" but which seem usable elsewhere in the magazine are turned over to the excerpt editor for consideration as filler material, and their contributors are so notified. Unless return postage is enclosed, all the anecdotes rejected as unacceptable are destroyed after consideration. At one time the Digest sent especially designed cards to every hopeful contributor to "Life in These United States," giving the editorial verdict on submitted material. This procedure had to be abandoned because of the sheer magnitude of the task. Some contributors had collected anywhere from a dozen to 100 of the cards. One also-ran who finally broke the tape wrote proudly that he owned a stack of 127.

The quality of the material which readers submit to "Life in These United States" is often high enough to make selection difficult. Americans have a well-developed sense of the ludicrous, a sharp eye, an ear for the comic in speech, an appreciation of the ridiculous. Many of them display a talent for seizing on the unusual and reporting it clearly. These are the stories that make the grade.

Unfunny vulgar stories, stories reflecting unpleasantly on an individual or a group do not get even the minimum two readings afforded all other contributions.

A stated requirement for acceptable contributions is that the story be true, out of the writer's personal experience, and unpublished. Unless the same things happen to hundreds of people living in widely separated places and happen every year, this restriction is often honored in the breach or at least liberally interpreted. The same stories, identical or told with only minor variations, reach the editors with monotonous regularity. Some of them were good the first time, perhaps even the tenth. They begin to look a little tired after that.

One which comes into the Digest periodically from all points of the compass the editors of "Life in These United States" have fondly dubbed "The Potted Child." The child is seated with his mother in a bus, streetcar, or subway. Over his or her head is a paper bag with holes cut in it for eyes and nose. The bag is knocked off, revealing a small head stuck firmly in a smaller child's pot. As the onlookers roar with laughter, the mother indignantly explains that she is taking the child to the doctor to have the crockery removed.

Another story has come in from every state. It seems now to be traveling the world, for the last version was received from Ceylon. A hostess is entertaining elaborately at a luncheon. Her pet steals or is given some of the rich delicacies prepared for her guests. Glancing out the window after the successful luncheon, the hostess sees the pet lying dead on the lawn. Horrified she telephones her doctor. She and her guests are rushed to the hospital and a stomach pump. As the exhausted hostess returns home, a neighbor, who had considerately waited until she knew the party would be over, apologizes for accidentally killing the pet with her car.

In August 1945 the Digest reprinted as "The Lasting Laugh" two pages of these chestnuts and perennials, hoping to dispose of them once and for all. The result was immediate demands from angry contributors for payments they considered due, even though the Digest had paid for and published each of the anecdotes before and had numerous versions of them all in its files.

One story sent the Digest shows not only the country's happy consciousness of "Life in These United States," but also how some of the repetitions may occur. A fascinated guest was zealously writing down some of the colorful talk of a cowboy guide at a dude ranch. He saw, guessed, and advised her not to bother. "Don't try to sell those to 'Life in These United States.' If I ever do think up anything good, *I* send it there. Mostly it's where I get my quaint sayings."

Though chosen for their editorial qualities and not for their geographical source or setting, anecdotes published in "Life in These United States" represent the length and breadth of the United States. An inquisitive Texan tabulated the entries for an 11-year period. Every state and region was covered. New York, especially New York City, led all the rest. California, Texas, Massachusetts, and Illinois provided the next most stories and story scenes. When the odds were posted by density of population, the most prolific sources were the District of Columbia, Wyoming, Vermont, Arizona, Idaho, California, New Hampshire, Utah, Montana, and Massachusetts—a fair spread with the South a bit weak.

In August 1957 the Digest published a matchless bit by a contributor who had tried and tried again without previously making "Life in These United States." What finally brought the writer through was this letter:

Dear Editor: Recently I sent a brief item to "Life in These United States," and after it was mailed remembered that I had not included my address. I wrote at once to correct the error.

Now I realize I wrote nothing in the second letter that would connect it with the first. Consequently, I'm asking you to forget the whole thing. The story wasn't very good anyway.

The delighted editors printed the letter with an italicized postscript: *"We think the foregoing letter is a classic, however, and would like to pay the contributor, but we can't read the signature —and there was no return address on this letter either!"*

Some readers wrote in asking if they had written the letter. They thought it sounded like them. Others wrote defending themselves. They always, they said, signed their names legibly and affixed their addresses. Some denied everything. One suggested that, if the names of claimants were to be drawn from a hat, he would like his included. Astounded when she read the letter in the Digest, the absent-minded wife of a college professor, who was not absent-minded at all, recognized herself and her handiwork, happily confessed, and got her $100 check.

CHAPTER XV

CONDENSED ARTICLES AND BOOKS

These standard and widely familiar departments of The Reader's Digest are important to the magazine. They are part of its recognizable individuality, and the Digest would be poorer without them. Yet they are incidental to the main body of the periodical which, instead of the original 30 or 31, is composed now of 40 to 45 articles, selected and condensed from other magazines or Digest originals, in each monthly issue.

What characterizes these articles and has characterized them since the inception of the Digest in 1922 is their freshness, vitality, variety, brevity, clarity—often their charm, often their provocativeness, often their humor. Chief characteristic of Digest articles, perhaps, is the readability which is the total of these and of all the other qualities which writers and editors strive to inject into them, and the accumulated experience with the magazine which readers bring to their reading of the articles.

The circulation of The Reader's Digest climbed rapidly and consistently from 1922 to 1930 and all through the 1930s. During World War II, with people avid for war news and comment and as eager for escape from the depressing actuality of the war, the circulations of almost all nationally distributed magazines rose greatly. The circulation of the Digest rose far more than most. It virtually doubled, from about 4,000,000 in 1941 to about 8,000,000 in 1946.

There was a shortage of magazine paper during the war years, but four copies of the pocket-sized Digest could be printed on about the same amount of paper that the larger magazines required for one, and the Digest, at that time, used no coated paper stock. By lessening the margins, a half inch was cut from the height of the magazine, with consequent additional saving of paper.

There was much military and necessary civilian travel during World War II. The portability of the Digest made it a convenient companion on trains, planes, and ships. Digest management saw to it that as many copies as could be printed were available in as many places as could be reached. A sailor could slip a copy into his sea bag; an army man could slip one under a shirt in his foot locker and still pass inspection. Copies of The Reader's Digest went with the troops everywhere, and during the war they were shipped overseas in large quantities to servicemen and women on every front.

Format, availability, and portability helped, but what chiefly accounted for the tremendous circulation growth of The Reader's Digest during and after World War II were the same qualities in the magazine that insured its initial success, quickly gave it mass circulation, and have since brought the Digest to its present commanding position.

During World War II its wide coverage of many subjects in compact form made The Reader's Digest a favorite in or out of the service. When you could carry or had time to read only one magazine, it appeared wisest to get the one which seemed to cover all the best of the others—*The Saturday Evening Post, Harper's, Collier's, Life, The New Yorker, American, American Mercury, Liberty, Argosy*—in one issue. If, overseas, the copy you got was six months old, it did not make much difference. The articles were not tied to a date. They were "articles of lasting interest." The familiar Digest looked like home to those overseas in the service. It had the look and feel of home. The jokes sounded like home.

The Digest did not make the mistake of turning itself wholly into a war journal. Men and women overseas wanted to read about natural and pleasant things at home. They had enough war on their hands. Often they resented some magazine pieces about the war by writers who, they felt, knew little or nothing of its realities. Readers at home wanted all the facts about the war and all the sound interpretations they could get, but they wanted to forget the war almost as badly as they wanted enlightenment about it. They too looked for the jokes, the adventure narratives, the personal-experience pieces, the medical articles, the animal stories.

The Reader's Digest, like the other national magazines, ran many serious war pieces. Some of its condensed books were thoughtful discussions, such as Walter Lippmann's *U.S. War Aims* in September 1944; William L. White's *Report on the Russians* in December 1944 and January 1945; Emory Reeves' *The Anatomy of Peace* in December 1945 and January 1946. Yet, often the condensed books in the wartime issues of The Reader's Digest were true-life adventure narratives, such as Jim Corbett's *Death of a Man-Eater* in September 1945 or Louise Baker's light and amusing *Party Line* in the same year.

Many of the war articles, in Digest fashion, were put in personal rather than objective terms. Some were as brutally realistic as a description of the wanton slaughter of American prisoners by German S.S. troops. Some were tales of high adventure with brutality enough included, like "I Was An American Spy," the first-person story of an American woman who ran a night club in Manila as a blind until she was discovered and tortured by the Japanese. Some were emotional and moving, as "They Walk Without Legs," or light and amusing, as "What English Girls Think of the Yankees" or "Are Yanks Lousy Lovers?" There were plenty of war stories of many kinds: "Glory Through Hara-Kari," a close-up of the Japanese fighting man; "Navy Heroes in Diving Suits"; "The Last Prussian," a biography of General Von Runstedt; "Jean Laffite—Pirate Patriot"; "Ernie Pyle's War"; "Our Wounded Come Home"; "War Orphans, U.S.A."; "Surgery in a Submarine."

At the same time there were the kind of Digest articles that might appear at any time, with the same bright diversity of subject and liveliness in the telling: "What We Can Learn from Children," "How To Pick a Mate," "Conquest of a Killer" (bacterial endocarditis) by Paul de Kruif, a warm story about Jim Thorpe, nature pieces by Donald Culross Peattie, "The Extraordinary Ways of Sir Thomas Beecham," and advice on "How to Swallow a Sword."

The same July 1943 issue of The Reader's Digest that opened with Max Eastman's warning, "We Must Face the Facts About Russia," carried an exposé of false cigarette advertising to which was appended the italicized editorial note: *"The Reader's Digest will publish from time to time reports on Federal Trade Commission proceedings against the manufacturers of other nationally advertised products.*" Among the articles which followed were a condensation of "The Day the Dam Broke" from James Thurber's *My Life and Hard Times* and a *New Yorker*-styled "profile" condensed from *Harper's* on "Harold Ross and *The New Yorker*" —Ross's acknowledgment was a five-part *New Yorker* burlesque on The Reader's Digest in the winter of 1945. This July 1943 Digest closed with a book condensation of Walter Lippmann's *U.S. Foreign Policy*, a serious analysis of its weaknesses and a plea for the formation of a sound and realistic policy.

In August 1943 the Digest's opening article was a warning by Henry J. Taylor titled "Boondoggling on a Global Basis." In the article Taylor warned of the dangers of exaggerated internationalism, which he described as being as "foolhardy and destructive as a narrow isolationism." Long before the Marshall Plan was devised, the Digest was warning against the impoverishment of the United States in fatuous planning for what was then being enthusiastically described as a "Better World Order." In the piece Taylor phrased what was almost heresy at the time: "The whole concept of giving or infusing the Four Freedoms universally is preposterous. It is not idealism. It is sheer political buncombe." In its political and social articles the Digest has seldom followed the paths of editorial expediency.

In February 1944 "Diasone: New Hope for White Plague Victims" got as much space as "The Real German Enemy" (the General Staff). "Sentinels of the Wild" by Archibald Rutledge got more space than "Chivalry in This War." "Cheering News on the Dental Front" got equal billing with "America's No. 1 Soldier," a biographical sketch of General George Catlett Marshall.

This balance of war and nonwar themes on the Digest's usual wide range of subjects is discernible throughout the Digests of war years. "How To Stay Young" and "Dr. Einstein on the Atomic Bomb" appeared in the same Digest with girls marrying by proxy in Kansas, American and British airmen tunneling their way out of Stalag Luft III in Sagan, Germany, and John Robert Powers revealing what makes a woman beautiful.

The November 1945 Digest opened with a thrilling first-person story of extraordinary adventure in New Guinea, "A WAC in Shangri-La," closed with a now-it-can-be-told piece, "The Silent, Invisible War Under the Sea." Between them were "Medicine's Newest Wonder Drug" (streptomycin), "Scarlet Pimpernels of the Air," a factual piece on *The Christian Science Monitor* condensed from *The Saturday Evening Post,* and a De Kruif description of Boss Kettering who, "despite heartbreaking disappointments . . . never admitted his goals were impossible—and he achieved them."

In the middle of the war the Digest, which ran reiterated warnings of what Soviet Russia was really like and of the dangers we might face in the postwar world through our own enthusiasm and naïveté, kept its eye on national affairs as well. Senator Joseph O'Mahoney's "America Is Being Made Over—and We Won't Like It," August 1943, was a warning of what was happening unnoticed in government at home. The article was a strong attack on government by executive order. Case histories of the interagency transfer of large sums of money and their expenditure for purposes which Congress had never intended were cited to show the number and danger of governmental actions of which the general public was largely unaware. ". . . it appears to reflect the purpose, in some government quarters, to make over our government in the ugly shape of totalitarianism which Congress and the people—if they were consulted—would emphatically repudiate."

The Reader's Digest publishes "Articles of Lasting Interest." DeWitt Wallace formulated the description when he began to publish his magazine. It was the test he applied in the selection of material for condensation and publication in the early years of the Digest. It still is. The phrase is repeated often in his conversation about the Digest, and it appears in print above the table of contents on the cover of every issue. The concept does not negate the timeliness which major Digest articles often display. The early pieces on Russia are a case in point, possibly also its descriptions of the dangers of a too enthusiastic and ill-considered internationalism. As early as February 1944 the Digest was pointing out the extent and effectiveness of education in Russia: "The Russian Slogan: 'Work, Study, and Learn.'"

Diversity with strong contrasts in appeal is a Digest mark at any time. In March 1946 the book condensation was *Jumper, the Life of a Siberian Horse* by Nicholas Kalashnikoff. "Among horse stories," read the editorial comment, "it may be compared to *Black Beauty* and *Smoky* in appeal to the human heart." The condensed book in April 1946 was *The Autobiography of Benjamin Franklin*. The Digest is never afraid of a people's classic. The condensed book in May 1946 was *The Snake Pit* by Mary Jane Ward, a vivid and terrifying account of life in a mental hospital. Some of the most popular book condensations in The Reader's Digest in recent years have been *A Man Against Insanity* by Paul de Kruif, *Born to Give* by Raymond B. Fosdick, *First Lady of the Seeing Eye*, as told to Blake Clark by Morris Frank, *While Others Sleep*, the story of the Strategic Air Command by James Michener, *The Adventures of Mark Twain* and *The Dog Who Wouldn't Be* by Farley Mowat—a mixed bag.

Medical articles generally command attention. Not unexpectedly, "I Was Afraid To Have a Baby" in April 1957 was among the most popular with women readers, though other medical articles, "How Your Blood Pressure Tells Your Story" in June 1956, "Doctors Should Tell Patients the Truth" in October 1956, and "Babies by Appointment" in July 1957, drew almost as many women readers. During the same period Paul Gallico's "Farewell to the Babe" (Didrikson) in January 1957 was slightly more popular than "What It Takes To Be a Queen" (Elizabeth II), which was featured in the issue for October 1957.

No Digest article since World War II provoked more furor than "The Facts Behind the Cigarette Controversy" by two Digest editors, Lois Mattox Miller and James Monahan, in July 1954. The article reviewed the findings of investigators who were attempting to find out how large a part smoking plays in the increase in lung cancer. Without exception the findings from tests and studies made by such institutions as the Memorial Center for Cancer and Allied Diseases in New York, the American Cancer Society, and the U. S. Public Health Service indicated close relationship. Medical authorities in France and Britain, as well as in the United States, were quoted to the same effect. It was a frightening article for many, including millions of smokers and the tobacco industry.

This article, which concluded only with the statement that each smoker would have to make up his mind for himself whether the psychological pleasures of the cigarette habit were worth the health risks involved, was followed by two articles in 1957, by the same authors, based on laboratory tests of filter-tip cigarettes.

They discovered that many filters did little to remove tars and nicotine, that some filter-tip cigarettes actually contained and transmitted more of them than some cigarettes without filters. These articles affected the consumer market for cigarettes and, depending on the habits, interests, and sympathies of the reader, aroused emotions ranging from conviction to consternation.

Sex in the classroom, the legal basis of the Nuremberg trials, a collection of old limericks, a rerun of "—And Sudden Death," get the children out of the jails, Elmer Sperry and his magic top, we must modernize Congress, bootleg nylons, wild wisdom, the American invasion of Britain, mealtime madness, diary of a Nazi girl, the new capitalism, how to keep ghosts out of town, labor is big business, the genius of Samuel Morse . . .

Because its material comes from varied sources, about one-half of it still reprinted from other periodicals, the Digest, unlike many other mass-circulation American magazines, has no recognizable "style." Though editorial selection and condensation give every article characteristic Digest simplicity and clarity, Digest styles are as various as the differing styles of the authors and the publications in which the material originally appeared and the differing approaches and mannerisms of the various roving editors and frequent Digest contributors.

The look of homogeneity is given the variety of the offering by format and type faces, by blending or complementary colored inks on cuts and legends, and by the titling. Digest titling has always been noteworthy. Its titles are consistently provocative, and for many years they have been supplemented by teasing subtitles which pique the reader's curiosity and urge him into the article. Currently these are more often "pretitles" than subtitles, generally preceding rather than following the title. Printed in roman if the title is in italics, or the reverse, or in a different type style or face, they are sometimes boxed or printed on a tint block. Position on the page of both title and subtitles is flexible rather than fixed, often flushed right or left rather than centered. Whatever the attention-getting device used, the words, as in all Digest matter, are more important than the auxiliary display.

Digest titles and subtitles make it difficult not to read what follows them.

Let the giver beware—last year 100 million dollars went into the pockets of unscrupulous promoters.

STOP THE "CHARITY" RACKETEER!

College troupe brings villains and vodvil back to the river

HERE COMES THE SHOWBOAT

A PRIVATE
FOREIGN-AID PROGRAM
THAT EARNS A PROFIT

Here is a going scheme that helps foreign nations to help themselves —and it doesn't cost U.S. taxpayers a cent

How the federal ban on wire-tap evidence protects spies and kidnapers

LET'S UNSHACKLE THE FBI

"If I Had My Life to Live Over—"

I'D PICK MORE DAISIES

I'D WANT MY HUSBAND TO MARRY AGAIN

Strange stories from jungle and field which pose the question

ARE ANIMALS REALLY "WILD"?

FOR THE KIDDIES TO READ

Many of the crime comics your children are exposed to are not just tales of violence but of perversion and depravity. Here's how one community cleansed its newsstands of this literary filth

THE STRANGE DEATH OF LOUIS SLOTIN

He was manipulating the elements of an A-bomb when his hand slipped —the long-withheld story of a scientist's duel with an invisible killer

Many travelers from abroad who must pass through the United States take home sorry memories. Often treated as suspects, held under armed guard, virtually incommunicado, they learn new facts about the land of the free

OUR SHABBY WELCOME TO FOREIGNERS

"Remember," says this stripper, "every customer is a sucker."

"I WORK IN A B-JOINT"

The most satisfying philosophy of life is the faith that here and the hereafter are one and the same

THERE IS NO DEATH

A noted minister and marriage counselor sheds some useful light on the eternal problem:

HOW TO LIVE WITH A WOMAN

How Hitler and his generals were fooled by one dead Englishman

THE CORPSE THAT HOAXED THE AXIS

Three solutions to the mystery of why some people rub you the wrong way

HATE AT FIRST SIGHT

What science knows about the magical processes of the human mind

WONDROUS STORAGE BATTERY—THE BRAIN

In any given year subjects of general interest and articles on literature, the arts and sciences account for more than half the editorial content of The Reader's Digest. National and foreign affairs together account for almost another quarter of the magazine. Though the nature of some of the articles and their impact on the public often give a different impression, articles on health and on business and industry—and these include Digest exposés and announcements of new drugs and cures—add up to little more than 10 per cent on the editorial content in most years. As with many of the other large-circulation magazines, travel is getting more attention in Digest pages than previously.

If one test of a magazine, as the test of a good book, is that it is in some way and to some degree a recognizable representation of life, The Reader's Digest can qualify. The Digest reflects many of the manifold aspects of life in enough of the manifold ways of looking at them.

CHAPTER XVI

FIRST-PERSON STORIES

In 1935 The Reader's Digest announced an article contest. Five prizes of $1000 each were offered for personal-experience stories. The response was so overwhelming that it nearly swamped the facilities which the magazine had at that time. A former editor of *The Bookman,* which had ceased publication shortly before, was hired. Working in a New York office, he and a staff of 7 assistants began to read and judge the competing articles.

One day, the editor in charge of the operation remembers, he had difficulty opening the office door. When he wedged himself inside he found the floor literally covered with newly arrived manuscripts. In the center stood a large apple barrel stuffed with excelsior. At the bottom was a single manuscript. Its author wanted his contribution noticed. Like the rest of the more than 43,000 manuscripts submitted, it was read at least twice. The winnowings were read three or four times.

In the end, ten instead of five $1000 prizes were awarded. Counting follow-ups on ideas suggested by some of the other manuscripts, the Digest got about twenty finished articles out of the contest. Almost all of the prize winners were autobiographical. The classic form has never lost its allure for the writer or its magazine appeal.

In February 1955 The Reader's Digest condensed "Protection for a Tough Racket" by Cordelia Baird Gross. It was a brightly told autobiographical tale of a substitute teacher in one of New York City's problem schools who took an after-hours job in a night club. The story had humor, pathos, neophyte gangsters in school, and a full-fledged scarface coming to the rescue of a damsel in distress in the classroom.

The Digest ran the piece with a boxed notice:

$2500 OFFERED
FOR
UNIQUE AND AUTHENTIC PERSONAL-EXPERIENCE STORIES
similar in quality and interest to
the foregoing article

The result this time was 18,999 stories submitted within the next four months, about 1500 manuscripts monthly ever since, and a further strengthening of the Digest's close relations with its readers. From February 1955 through November 1957 nearly 70,000 first-person stories reached the Digest, including 1723 from Australia, 2352 from Canada, and 4814 from England. Out of the 70,000 the Digest published just 35. The chances are slim, but the reward, twenty-five times that for a chosen bit in "Life in These United States," is high. It has been high enough to attract the professional as well as the amateur, and about half the published stories have been by writers or prominent people.

The first story published as a result of the competition was "My Japanese Brother" by William Jennings Bryan, Jr., which appeared in June 1955. *The Saturday Evening Post* veteran, Nina Wilcox Putnam, was in by February 1956 with "The Day

I Went Fishing with Grover Cleveland." Mary Ellen Chase made it with "Are You Afraid of Snakes?"; Jerome Weidman with "The Night I Met Einstein," and Brig. Gen. Robert L. Scott, Jr., with "Unscheduled Operation." Other writers have won the first-person award, but successful competitors have included school-teachers, a sea captain, professors, doctors, engineers, a housewife, generals of the Army and the Air Force, public officials, and a woman therapist.

The requirement is that each be a "true narrative of a personal experience in some specialized walk of life—dramatic, inspirational, humorous—and especially revelatory of human nature." Many, in Digest fashion, have reduced to reverent appreciation of the ennobling humility of the great—a President being kind to a little girl, a great scientist teaching a callow young man to enjoy Bach—but characters, setting, and moral have ranged widely. "The Day I Met Caruso" was pure inspiration and sentiment, and again the great man, but "The First Big Radio Broadcast" simply described that historic event which took place at Boyle's Thirty Acres in Jersey City when Jack Dempsey fought Georges Carpentier, July 2, 1921. "The Day I Met Midnight" was a cowboy's taming of an outlaw horse. "Baggy Pants" was what happened when Japanese guards seized the secret writing of a captive U.S. general. "In the Eye of the Hurricane" is explained by its title, but "The Great Molasses Flood" was something else again. The bursting of a storage tank flooded South Boston with the gluey stuff. "He Never Asked That a Thing Be Easy" was subtitled, "Larry couldn't walk, he could barely talk, but what a gift of the spirit he brought to others."

First-person stories carry one step further the Digest policy of inviting reader participation in the conduct of the magazine. Like "Life in These United States," "Life in This Wide World,"

"Humor in Uniform" (which draws an average of 3000 contributions a month), "Personal Glimpses," "Toward a More Picturesque Speech," "Laughter, the Best Medicine," they provide a direct channel for reverse communication between the reader and the Digest. There is the stimulus this time of very substantial monetary reward and the even more open and valuable invitation to talk about one's self. Many contributors, even among the vast majority whose manuscripts have been rejected, have written the Digest that the attempt to write out in story form some episode of especial significance in their lives was a reward in itself. It intensified meaning and enriched the experience for them, giving them some of the joy of creation and enhancing their appreciation of those stories in the Digest which show the story qualities for which they strove.

Like any such competition, the first-person story serves to strengthen the emotional ties between reader and magazine, deepening realization of the values of the periodical. The device acts as a good-will gesture and a strong circulation builder.

From the editorial viewpoint, the first-person story has an even more essential value. As one contributor wrote, after having expressed his pleasure in the opportunity afforded him and the pleasure felt in the effort even though he had failed, "Quite possibly you may disclose hidden treasures which might have been buried forever without your encouragement." This is part of the Digest's attempt and, again, typical of the Digest's fundamental approach to its audience and to its material. The first-person story provides a way of reaching out beyond the usual channels of journalism into life itself for vital stories by those who have actually lived them. The results have justified the expectations of the editors by providing real-life adventure of varied kinds with the thrills and inspiration that the Digest seeks out and publishes in both its selected and condensed and original articles.

In "Once 'Executed,' He Came Back to Save a Nation" a Guatemalan doctor told of the machine-gun massacre of 26 patriots by a dictator's zealous assassins. The bodies were stacked in army ambulances and dumped in the charnel-house morgue of a hospital. Incredibly the doctors found three of the men still alive. Risking their own lives, they worked to save them. One of these men, though recaptured, imprisoned, and tortured, survived to become the democratically elected president of Guatemala. "I Saw a Historic Blood Transfusion," by a surgeon and diplomat who had been minister to Panama and became the first United States ambassador to Venezuela, described a miracle of another kind. "I Knew Those Wright Brothers Were Crazy" told the story of a spectator whose convictions were shattered by that first flight at Kittyhawk. A Yankee newspaper editor and his bride fought corruption in San Juan. A crippled boy taught courage to his teacher and classmates. In "The Two-edged Dagger of Yusof Hussein" an RAF pilot described adventure behind enemy lines in Burma. A musical-comedy actress described her harrowing experience in the Iroquois Theater fire in Chicago in 1903.

The stories differ widely, but all are gripping, vital—and personal. Heroism and danger, spiritual as well as physical courage, miracles in out-of-the-way places of the world or just over the doorstep at home are their ingredients. In this they are typical Reader's Digest stories. They stir with epic drama, provoke a lyric sympathy, uplift, inspire. In the reactions they produce they are also typical Digest human-interest pieces. Occasionally a first-person story produces unexpected and far-reaching results, effects demonstrable in terms of human happiness.

In the Digest for January 1957 the first-person story was "America Seems Near to Me Now." Written by Mutsumi Kurahashi, a young farm girl on a remote island of Japan, it told poignantly of a family's deep happiness when a war diary taken from the body of a dead Japanese corporal on New Guinea was returned by an American veteran of the war in the South Pacific. The returned diary was placed on the family's Buddhist prayer shelf and a bowl of freshly boiled rice placed beside it every day.

After the story the Digest ran a note addressed to veterans of Pacific combat in World War II: "If you have among your souvenirs a Japanese diary and wish to make some family in Japan as happy as the American soldier mentioned in the foregoing article made the Kurahashi family . . . simply send the diary with your name and address to: First-Person Editor." The diary would be forwarded to Tokyo and every effort would be made to return it to the family concerned. In response to this appeal for the return of other Japanese war diaries as "a generous gesture of international good will," 137 war mementos were sent the first-person editors. The Reader's Digest, through its Tokyo offices, and Japanese authorities sought out the families concerned and notified them that an article belonging to their dead son or father had been returned.

The families, many of them humble people from remote districts who had to travel several days and nights to reach the office of the governor or the prefectural center where the mementos were formally returned, were deeply grateful. Their letters of thanks to American veterans of World War II who had returned diaries or personal papers, sometimes only an address list or a car license, are among the most poignant The Reader's Digest has ever received.

The excerpts quoted here tell their own story and make their own comments.

Fourteen years has gone by since I learned of the death of my eldest son Kazuo by an official notice. For these years I have not lived a single day without thoughts of him. "Killed in action at Guam" was all that was given. . . . It was too sudden a joy for me to receive the souvenirs. To have a thing that belonged to Kazuo out of the limited number of discovered mementos of Japanese soldiers . . . is indeed a miraculous dispensation. . . . Though I have never seen you, I feel the warmth of your heart. My son's soul now, I am sure, rests in peace with all the 28 years' memory of his young life.

Another mother wrote out of emotions sharpened by relief from bitterness.

For these thirteen years the visage of my dead son has been haunting me and constant thoughts of him and sorrows have been eating my heart, but now all tormenting feelings are gone from my heart thanks to your kind deed.

In those dark days of war we were taught to give up everything for the country in the name of the country. It was patriotic and the best expression of filial piety to die in the battlefields.

But when the war was over, the loss of lives seemed the only reality and price we paid we did not know what for. Even today only a nominal sum is paid by the government for this terrible sacrifice we had to make. An official communication said "the remains of your son have arrived," and we hurried over only to find a handful of dust in a wooden box. They made fools of those who died in the war.

But the rancor and black despair have been suddenly lifted from my heart when my son's actual possession was brought to me through the good offices of the Japan branch of The Reader's Digest. We thank you deeply. . . . This article at least is not a lie, my son was carrying it around with him; it brings back to us his image with it. We are with him now. God bless you. . . .

I recall the days when the war was terminated [another woman wrote]. *Soldiers were beginning to come back. We hungrily looked for his name in the list of returning soldiers of the radio corps.*

They never found it.

When we finally had to give up hope, my husband was quite a broken man. Even the ash tray which our son used to use became the object of his possessive love; he guarded over it jealously and hid it somewhere to keep it away from the gaze and touch of others. The taciturn man became more silent; enduring desolation of life to his last, he died 5 years ago. I have reported the joyful news to him and I know he is now sleeping his eternal sleep in happiness together with his beloved. . . . As I had always dreamed, my beloved child is at last back with me. I shall never let him go from now on. I feel he is back to watch over me, to strengthen me to live bravely in old age, and I feel I have the strength now.

This letter came from a wife whose son was an infant when the husband left for the army.

It was an evil war. Both your side and ours, the conqueror and the conquered, have lost innumerable lives of our relations and loved ones. We know the terrible nature of war, and we must do everything not to let it happen again. . . . I have not forgotten the terrible sting of sorrow I had felt in learning of his death and am busily engaged in our family trade, dairy farming. . . . We have placed the souvenir on the family altar; in looking at this souvenir, I seem to have the definite notion of my husband's death for the first time in my life. I shan't be moping over it any more. Seeing his visage in our son's, I am not unhappy. . . .

This girl child was an infant when her father went into the Japanese army.

I have never known my father's voice. I only knew him by the picture placed on the altar. But I can now hear his voice from the words written in his notebook. My sweet father of whom I have heard so much from my mother is right here with me. I call out to him in a whisper saying, this is your daughter Miyuki. And it was you who brightened my melancholy heart by bringing to life my father's memory.

A sister wrote:

We have only your generosity to thank for this souvenir of my brother. The small address book he was carrying about with him no doubt to his last went to his father, his mother being dead for the past years. He was so happy having it and said that it gave him the momentary illusion of his son back with him. I saw him join the palms in thanks to you.

A woman who had received neither the symbolic remains nor any article belonging to a son killed in action had only been able to observe the official death date by having Buddhist masses read monthly and yearly and praying daily for the repose of his soul. The diary was handed to her by the editor of the Japanese edition of The Reader's Digest in the governor's office.

That was a moment of much emotion for me. Tears of sorrow and happiness gushed out to confuse me. . . . Such a thing, I am afraid, could only be understood by one who has lost his father or brother or her husband by the war. Upon return home, I promptly placed the diary before the tablet of the deceased and amidst burnt incense and freshly cut flowers, I reported the matter to him and prayed for him. My son, I am sure, was happy to hear it.

Bitter memories of the war and heartfelt hopes that its tragedies would never be repeated appear in many of the letters. This one came from the family of a Japanese flier who was lost in the Marshall Islands in December 1943.

Nothing of his remains or his belongings reached me and we had only his picture to pray to.

A simple verse well current in this country those days sums up the military precept inculcated in every one of us; it goes something like this: "I am prepared to die in the sea or in the mountain serving the cause of our Emperor." Young boys fought and died without regret because of such education. What took place 12 years ago comes back to me like yesterday's event.

I have no word but thanks to you for preserving for 12 long years a possession of an enemy soldier whom you have never known. I have heard you live in New Jersey and have acquainted myself with the place on a map of America.

In the extensive raids on the Japanese main island we were bombed out. We had nothing left but our own selves to start out with. We bore it all for the country. But everything was futile and we have none to blame but the war itself for the miseries we went through.

Emerging finally from the debris of war, we made a vow to ourselves that from now on we do everything to spare future humanity the tragedy we have known. I know all Americans feel the same.

One surprised member of the Japanese Air Corps, now piloting a surburban train past the rice paddies, received his army notebook. He had fought at Borneo and Tinian and was transferred from Guam a few days before annihilation of the Japanese forces there. The end of the war found 7000 Japanese soldiers at a base cut off from all supplies. "We had to catch jungle rats and lizards to eat and live. Only a handful of us lived to see Japan. . . . As a survivor, I mourn all servicemen of America and Japan who made the supreme sacrifice and want to dedicate the rest of my life to the construction of a warless world, as one of the laborers."

As moving as these letters are, they are no more poignant and revealing than the staccato jottings of a Lieutenant Tabei, whose diary contained a factual account of the action on Guadalcanal until his death in action. So important was this document considered that on its return the full contents were made available to the Japanese press and radio.

January 1, Friday, 1943: "Got up at 4 A.M. *At 6 all men still able to walk stood in a line, led by the battalion commander, observed New Year sunrise and gave three cheers to the Emperor. . . .*

New Year observed in Guadalcanal under most wretched circumstances. It will do me well to remember this unique experience of destitution in my life and let it serve as a useful guidance for future.

In the middle of our New Year's rites observed in homage of the Emperor from a distance, a large formation of enemy bombers spun overhead in a great demonstration. I resent this. . . .

The Japanese troops were so weakened by malaria that they were unable to fight. Planned attacks were canceled. The enemy, Tabei wrote, was everywhere. He and his men were without supplies. He was wounded in the right hand and "the rear part."

January 11. Orderly Yamanaka hit and killed. This is heartbreaking. We had shared everything, life and the risks. 11 men remain now with me.

The American attack increased in power and destruction. The promised planes that were the only hope of thousands and thousands of Japanese did not appear. More U.S. troops landed, and a savage naval bombardment struck the Japanese from the sea. Japanese casualties were frightful. Tabei, his own command wiped out, was placed at the head of a special hand-combat group. January twenty-first he made the final entry in his diary.

Exhausted from yesterday's heavy rain, but am determined to live through to the end with sheer spiritual energy. The score getting worse, the enemy trench mortars concentrating fire on us. At this writing, 13:00. Perhaps I'll be alive tomorrow to continue this diary, perhaps not. Only Providence can decide that. Father and Mother sleep tight.

CHAPTER XVII

ART WORK AND PHOTOGRAPHY

The Reader's Digest is a text magazine, meant to be read. It is not a pictorial magazine meant primarily to be looked at. For 17 years after its founding the Digest was solely a text magazine. The first black-and-white illustrations appeared in November 1939.

Even today The Reader's Digest is not what is usually considered an illustrated magazine. There are no half-tone black-and-white reproductions in its editorial section, nor is there often use of color photography inside the issue on the editorial pages. The antique paper stock used on most Digest editorial pages does not permit use of such illustrative material. Since the Digest began to accept advertising in April 1955 and to use glossy paper for its advertising pages and part of the editorial, half tones and full-color photography have been used in the advertisements but only occasionally elsewhere in the issue.

Line drawings in black and white were introduced in Digest pages in 1939, but their use was limited until a general typographical redesigning of The Reader's Digest was begun with the issue for July 1945. In 1948, with a shift in printing to especially designed Goss presses, the Digest began to use illustrations in color. These are printed not from the usual four-color plates but through using four line plates in selected colors along with a single black key plate to obtain a multicolored effect. With the admission of advertising to The Reader's Digest and the appearance of color and striking illustrations in the advertising pages, the Digest began to use larger illustrations, more color, additional white space, and to try for more striking typographical effects.

Pictures accompanying Reader's Digest condensed articles are designed to highlight and dramatize a point of central interest in the narrative which is usually part of a Digest article. These are varied with black-and-white portraits of people, occasionally, where the article permits such treatment, of birds or animals. They are printed without captions. Outside artists are commissioned to do these pictures, often with treatments and subsequent changes suggested by the Digest's art department in order to obtain desired effects.

They are meant to enhance article interest and not merely to appear as decorations. This is a usual art editor's intent and, if the pictures are successful, part of his accomplishment. In addition, Digest illustrations are meant to complement the style and treatment of the text matter. They must be clear and understandable to the many, not complicated expressions of artistic virtuosity for appreciation by the few. Digest illustrations, like the Digest itself, are for everyman, not for the *cognoscenti.* Some posterized Digest illustrations have a simplicity that approaches the primitive. The attempt is to reach the average human being with art that he will understand and enjoy. To realize this end in the Digest, as C. O. Woodbury, its art editor, phrases it, "We work on many different kinds of paper with many kinds of tools to get many different effects." There are 25 to 30 illustrations, ranging from major pictures to vignettes and spots, in a typical current issue of The Reader's Digest.

Digest covers are another matter, and here the art work is of two contrasting kinds, one used on the United States and the other used on the various foreign editions of the magazine.

For the first few years of its existence The Reader's Digest was a severe black and white, even on its covers, which were not distinguished in paper stock or by more than a printer's ornament from the inside pages of the book-appearing magazine. A heavier cover stock was introduced when the table of contents was shifted to the front cover. At the same time the use of color was introduced. The color was in the cover stock, which continued to be overprinted in black. Actual color printing was not used on Digest covers until a decorative panel was inserted in the left-hand margin of the table of contents. Small decorative pictures were used at first. In 1948 the Digest began to use wrap-around cover paintings, part of which appears on the front-cover panel, most of which overflows to spread over the entire back cover. The back cover must present a complete picture in itself, but the whole must blend into one unified composition when the magazine is opened flat. In 1957 the Digest began to experiment with placing the table of contents on the back cover and using a whole picture, with boxed logotype inset, on the front.

Reader's Digest covers for the domestic edition began with a series of paintings of the shrines of America. They have continued to depict scenes from American life, country and city scenes, agricultural, industrial—a broad selection of pictorial Americana.

For these covers sketches are prepared. Certain of the sketch ideas are approved after critical scrutiny and put into comprehensive form for consideration by the art directors and interested editors of the Digest. Finished water colors are painted from those which are approved. A few of these cover paintings are executed within the Digest's own art department, but most are commissioned from ranking American and English water colorists. Mrs. Wallace makes the final selection, choosing from among many finished water colors those which will be used as Reader's Digest covers.

Art work of the same general type used in the domestic edition of The Reader's Digest is used in the distinctively designed quarterly volumes issued by The Reader's Digest Condensed Book Club. Mrs. Wallace has been actively interested from the beginning in the design and packaging of the books, her objective being a book beauty and elegance which will make the volumes pleasant to see, handle, and enjoy as objects in themselves as well as pleasurable to read. Again, specifications for the illustrations used in these books include the capturing of some dramatic action of the story so that pictorialization, without captions, will add an additional interest to the text. Each volume contains 40 to 50 pictures by American and English illustrators. Some 1500 pictures have been commissioned and purchased since 1950 for Digest books alone. Final selection of covers for the Condensed Books, for Digest covers and the Digest Christmas card, which goes each year to the millions who receive gift subscriptions, is made by Lila Acheson Wallace.

It would be difficult, perhaps impossible, to isolate for analysis the work of Lila Bell Acheson Wallace at The Reader's Digest. Hers is a pervasive influence. Manuscripts do not bear her notes and comments, but some of the critical appraisal of important

Digest pieces has undoubtedly stemmed from her reading. Mrs. Wallace was wholly responsible for the book condensations of *Bambi* and *Little Boy Lost. Cry, the Beloved Country* was published on her recommendation. It was she who suggested the Digest article series on art and the book condensation in February 1955 of Joan Henry's *Yield to the Night*. Her presence permeates the Digest structure. Her ideas may often be reflected through DeWitt Wallace, but her taste is manifested everywhere—in the landscaping of the Digest grounds, in the décor of the Digest offices, guesthouse, and High Winds, and in The Reader's Digest Collection of Fine Arts. Digest workers who may never have seen her are surrounded during the working day by evidences of her taste. Readers of the Digest and of the Condensed Books are affected by that same taste as evidenced in the art work of the magazine and the books. Since 1954, in addition to her Digest work, Lila Acheson Wallace has been a director of the New York Central Railroad Company. She was elected to the board both for her abilities as an organizer and administrator and to bring a woman's taste and viewpoint to the making of corporate decisions.

Not art work but color photography is used, and has been used since the mid-1940s, on the covers of the International Editions of The Reader's Digest. In its New York offices the Digest has a collection of some 30,000 color negatives depicting the scenic beauty, national monuments, architecture, and people and their customs in most of the major countries of the world. It is probably one of the largest such collections extant. All of these pictures were taken by Digest staff photographers in an effort to obtain the best possible shots for reproduction on the covers of the various International Editions of The Reader's Digest.

Color cover pictures were first used by *Selecciones del Reader's*

Digest, the Spanish-language edition which circulates in South America. As readers showed their liking for the photographs, the experiment was extended so that the use of color photographs on their covers is now the general practice of all the International Editions of The Reader's Digest—a practice which requires the use of more than 250 different color cover photographs every year, in contrast to the 12 or 52 used by the leading pictorial magazines of the United States.

The job of providing covers for each of the International Editions every month in the year soon proved the impossibility of dependence upon standard commercial sources of supply. In 1948 the Digest began to shoot its own color photographs. A photographic laboratory and darkroom were set up in the Digest's New York art department, and a photographer was dispatched to Europe. Another photographer was added, and soon one man was spending six months of the year in the field, then spelling his alternate in the laboratory so that he could make additional photographic trips and maintain liaison with the editors of the International Editions to know their specific pictorial requirements.

Digest photographers have visited more than 40 countries in their search for new and unusual cover material. A photographer usually spends two weeks in each country, endeavoring to choose a different time of year for each visit so the resulting pictures will have seasonal variety. Working a seven-day week in the field, he follows a shooting schedule prepared in advance by the editorial offices of each foreign edition, a schedule worked up by locations and picture possibilities. Necessary permissions have been obtained and number of indoor subjects arranged in case the photographer should run into days of bad weather.

After experimenting with other equipment, Digest photographers settled on the 3″ x 5″ camera. Ninety per cent of Digest photographic covers have been produced from transparencies this size or larger, though 35-mm. shots can be used if the pictures are perfect and sharp enough to be blown up. Outdoor film with blue flash bulbs is used for both interior and exterior shots. Eight or ten shots are made of every subject from various exposures to insure that at least one will be perfect, since the photographer may be a thousand miles from the scene by the time the print is developed. Exposed film is then airmailed to New York, where it is processed in the Digest's laboratories. After the transparencies have been mounted, a cover meeting is held in New York with Digest editors reviewing each picture and selecting the best on each subject for possible cover use. Transparencies are then sent to the Digest editor in the country where they were taken. From these that editor makes his selection of cover pictures for the coming year.

Because of its greater distance from the United States, the shooting schedule for Japan varies from that for countries in Europe. Digest photographers visit Japan only every three years but remain there for several months, shooting enough pictures to supply the Japanese editions with color covers until their next visit.

Primary requisite for the color photograph to serve as cover of one of the Digest's International Editions is that it arouse a sense of pride in the national for whom it is intended. It may show the natural beauty of his country, recall its past glory, point to its achievements. Editors and photographers can choose from a wealth of possibilities to achieve this end—industry, science, education, monuments, arts, crafts, or symbolic composites of coins, pottery, medals, flowers. Occasionally a subject of universal interest fits the requirements for more than one International

Edition of The Reader's Digest. A popular and successful cover used by most of them was a color photograph of the United Nations building in New York at sunset. The most popular cover, internationally, is a landscape with sun and water and children at play.

Digest photographers have little trouble shooting in the United States. Seemingly everyone is happy to pose, and publicity-conscious manufacturers compete to have their products shown in pictures. In England and on the Continent they meet with reluctance from both individuals and industry. A manufacturer in Holland angrily refused to allow photographing of the clay pipes produced in his plant. A potter in England would not permit photographing of the fine bone china he made. Because of the number of permissions required from a half dozen authorities before a photographer can shoot in a park, a palace, or a cathedral, England is the most difficult of all the countries which the Digest covers in which to take pictures. The American cover-girl tradition does not hold in Spain. There, where a young lady may never be seen in public without her duenna, girls consider it vulgar to have their pictures appear in the public print, and permission to photograph them is never granted.

More strenuous objections are sometimes encountered. A Digest photographer who was taking pictures of copper mining in communist northern Finland was headlined in the local newspaper as an American spy. The same newspaper had earlier decided that a group of visiting German boy scouts were also spies. Its account complained that the democracies which had first sent juveniles in shorts were now using adult agents in trousers.

Digest covers, whether water colors for the domestic or full-color photographs for the foreign editions, are chosen, like the illustrations inside the magazine and those in Reader's Digest Condensed Books, for their universality of appeal. They are not for those educated to critical appreciation of the graphic arts. They are for the millions.

A Raoul Dufy in The Reader's Digest Collection.

The Reader's Digest is a multilingual, multinational magazine read on every continent.

A British edition of The Reader's Digest was founded in 1938. The first foreign-language edition, *Selecciones del Reader's Digest* for Spanish America, was inaugurated in December of 1940.

BARNELL

The South Sea lounge at the Digest.

WANN

A reception room in the business offices of The Reader's Digest combines traditional elegance with relaxed informality.

F

An unusual effect obtained thro
an unusual mural painting.

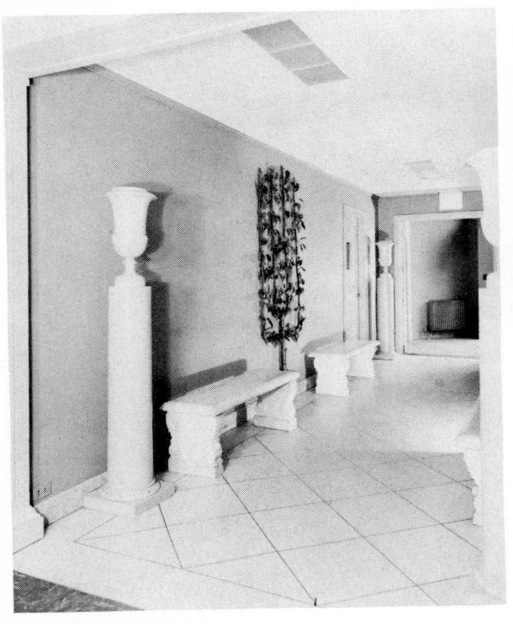

Marble for a touch of classical
trast in one of the entrance
Chappaqua.

GOTTSCHO-SCHLEISNER

Lawns and formal gardens about the offices of The Reader's Digest. The magazine has won numerous awards for its industrial landscaping.

ntique sundial in a orner of the Digest's ardens.

A delightful balcony overlooks another part of the extensive plantings about the grounds of the Digest's headquarters in northern Westchester County.

FORBERT

A Utrillo in The Reader's Digest Collection.

A Bonnard in The Reader's Digest Collection.

Published in 30 editions in 13 different languages, The Reader's Digest is read in every major country in the free world.

The International Editions of The Reader's Digest—in Arabic and Japanese, in English, French, Spanish, Portuguese, in Swedish, German, Italian, Danish, Norwegian, Finnish, and Dutch—are read by millions on millions of readers abroad. The Digest's condensed articles and books, its humor and human interest provide information, inspiration, and entertainment to many people in many lands.

Through its International Editions, The Reader's Digest has uncovered a world-wide community of interest, finding that people of whatever nationality and language respond to the same subjects of basic human appeal. Articles on education, self-help, achievement in the face of odds, on health and on the art of living are read as eagerly in Germany and Japan as in the United States.

Every month The Reader's Digest presents its own picture of America and Americans to the rest of the world with a clarity and warmth which cannot usually be achieved through the official channels of international relations.

Everything which appears in any of the International Editions has first appeared in the domestic edition of The Reader's Digest, but the contents of every International Edition are selected by its own editorial staff in the country for which it is published, and the magazine is likewise printed and distributed in that country by its own nationals.

The late Barclay Acheson, brother of Mrs. Wallace, who had been Secretary of Near East Relief, founded many of the foreign-language editions of the Digest. He served as the first Director of International Editions, 1942-1957.

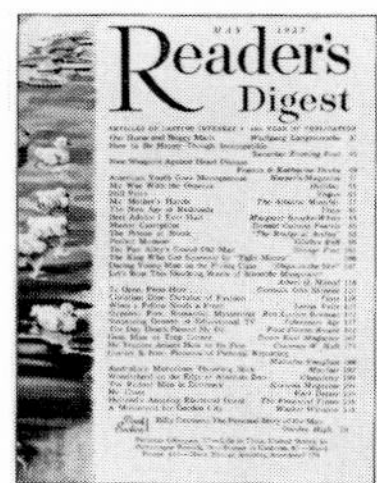

★ ENGLISH

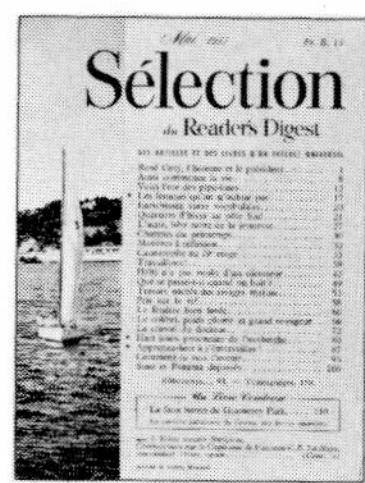

★ FRENCH

★ SPANISH

★ PORTUGUESE

★ DANISH

★ NORWEGIAN

★ ARABIC

★ FINNISH

THIRTEEN DIFFERENT LANGUAGES

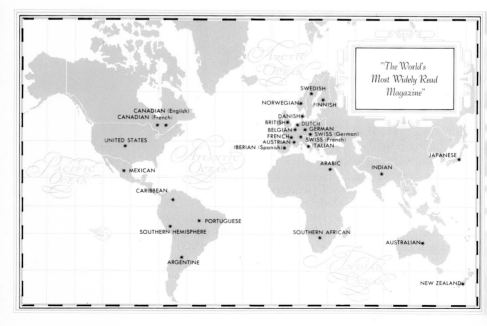

"The World's Most Widely Read Magazine"

ARCTIC OCEAN

ATLANTIC OCEAN

PACIFIC OCEAN

INDIAN OCEAN

SWEDISH
NORWEGIAN
FINNISH
DANISH
BRITISH
DUTCH
BELGIAN
GERMAN
FRENCH
SWISS (German)
AUSTRIAN
SWISS (French)
IBERIAN (Spanish)
ITALIAN
CANADIAN (English)
CANADIAN (French)
UNITED STATES
MEXICAN
CARIBBEAN
PORTUGUESE
SOUTHERN HEMISPHERE
ARGENTINE
ARABIC
INDIAN
JAPANESE
SOUTHERN AFRICAN
AUSTRALIAN
NEW ZEALAND

★ JAPANESE

★ GERMAN

★ ITALIAN

BARNELL

★ DUTCH

A Digest photograph of the Italian Riviera. Where water colors by well-known American and English artists are used on covers of the domestic edition of The Reader's Digest, color photographs are used for the covers of the International Editions. Digest staff photographers travel the world in search of pictures showing the scenic beauty, national monuments, and characteristic architecture of various countries which will serve as colorful and symbolic covers for specific foreign-language editions. More than 250 different covers are used each year. The Reader's Digest has a collection of more than 30,000 color negatives depicting scenes, people, and places in more than 40 different countries, all gathered in its continuous search for significant and meaningful covers and illustrations for its International Editions.

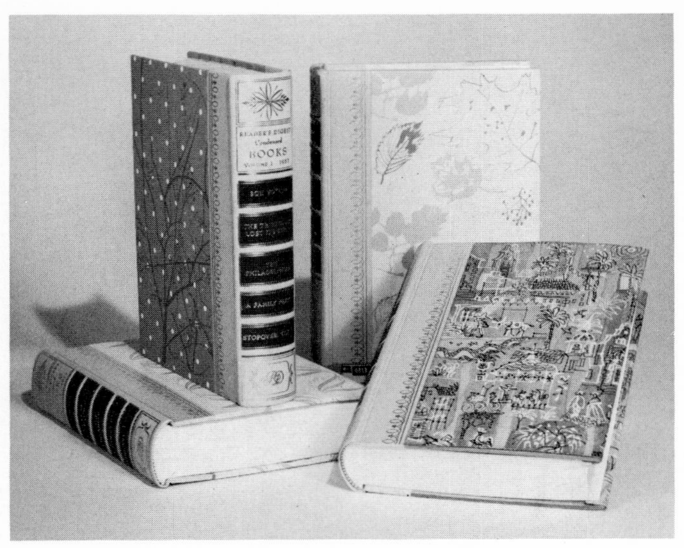

The Reader's Digest Condensed Book Club issued its first volume in the spring of 1950.

The popularity of condensed books in The Reader's Digest provoked a reader demand for more. The Reader's Digest Condensed Book Club, which issues quarterly volumes of about 575 pages each, was founded as a result.

Each volume contains condensations of four or five current books which have been condensed in The Reader's Digest itself. Usually there are condensations of two or more long novels, together with condensations of shorter nonfiction books.

The volumes are of the same general format, but each is distinctively bound and profusely illustrated in color to bring readers books that are esthetically pleasing as well as enjoyable to read.

CHAPTER XVIII

INTERNATIONAL EDITIONS

An English edition of The Reader's Digest, inaugurated in 1938, was immediately successful. It quickly reached the largest circulation of all monthly shilling magazines published in the British Isles.

A Spanish-language edition for Central and South America had been considered, but the idea had been abandoned when a survey showed the costs prohibitive. It was reintroduced in 1940, when Axis infiltration of South America made counteraction of the kind the Digest could provide seem advisable. The same objections held. There was no organized system of magazine distribution, and, with the low income levels of many of the countries, people could not pay the Digest cover price. It was A. L. Cole who suggested that the price be halved and the Spanish edition be opened to advertising. The Wallaces agreed, expecting to meet the remaining deficit themselves.

The Reader's Digest for August 1940 carried a four-page insert bordered with the flags of the United States and the 20 republics of Latin America. In announcing the Digest's first foreign-language edition, DeWitt Wallace wrote: "Letters from all over the world tell us that The Reader's Digest is a most effective interpreter of the United States to those living in other countries. . . . Readers everywhere join in emphasizing the need for extending the interpretative influence of The Reader's Digest throughout those countries where a clear conception of the United States of today will promote an alliance of interests for the cause of peace tomorrow."

A sale of about 20,000 copies was forecast, with 50,000 the most optimistic prediction. Instead the entire press run of 125,000 copies of the first issue of *Selecciones del Reader's Digest* was sold out. Within a year Argentina, which had been persuaded to take 25,000 copies of that first issue, was selling 75,000. Mexico jumped from 9000 to 31,000; Chile from 10,000 to 36,000; Peru from 3000 to 16,000. Colombia and Ecuador showed comparable multiplication. The advertising of large United States companies selling in Central and South America came into the magazine. There was no monetary deficit for the Digest to absorb.

Two years later, when the Spanish edition of The Reader's Digest had an average monthly circulation of 400,000, the Digest began publication of a Portuguese edition, which other readers in South America had demanded, *Seleções do Reader's Digest*. It was even more quickly successful than its predecessor. Brazilians bought more copies of the first issue than all the Spanish-speaking countries had bought of *Selecciones*. A year later the monthly circulation of the Portuguese edition was 300,000, with 37,000 each month going to Portugal itself.

Late in the war year of 1942 the Office of War Information approached The Reader's Digest with a request that it be allowed to reprint the magazine in neutral Sweden. Permission to use the Digest in this way for propaganda purposes was flatly and firmly refused, but a counterproposal was made. The Digest itself would explore the possibility of publishing a Swedish edition.

Barclay Acheson, made director of International Editions that year, and Marvin Lowes, who had helped found the English edition and who had remained in England for three years in charge of it, started overseas immediately. They were in the rear smoking compartment when their plane crashed off Newfoundland and broke in two. Twelve passengers forward were lost. Acheson and Lowes were flown back to the United States, where they caught another plane for Sweden. They interviewed 150 translators in Sweden from whom they picked an editor as well as the first translator. Though Nazi Germany tried to block the move, *Det Basta ur Reader's Digest* appeared on the newsstands of Sweden in March 1943. To meet the swift demand for copies, the first issue had to be twice reprinted. By the close of World War II circulation of the Swedish edition of The Reader's Digest, in a country of only 6,000,000 people, had reached 235,000 a month.

An Arabic edition of the Digest was also instituted in 1943 at the urging of OWI. Publication, which ceased in 1947, was re-instituted in 1956.

New foreign editions of The Reader's Digest came swiftly after the close of World War II, in many cases at the urging of readers in the countries for which they are published and in some instances—including Egypt and Italy—at the direct request of governmental officials in those countries.

Acheson and Lowes visited the countries where new editions were contemplated, staying usually one or two months. During this time they interviewed editorial and business people and, where publication was decided upon, selected a small staff. They checked the sale of local magazines, investigated distribution facilities, and built up what additional facilities were necessary. Often a new foreign edition of The Reader's Digest had its beginnings in a smoke-filled hotel room with a calculating machine borrowed from the hotel's office to do the first rough figuring.

In later years Acheson and Lowes, who is now assistant director of International Editions, were accompanied by a production man and a financial man on their exploratory expeditions which usually resulted in the founding of a new foreign edition of The Reader's Digest. A group composed of editorial, financial, circulation, and production men, who act independently, now operate throughout the year, visiting and checking in the various Digest offices abroad, transmitting the experiences of the domestic edition of the Digest and of all the other International Editions to the office being visited.

Brig. Gen. Paul W. Thompson, one of the youngest ground-forces generals in World War II, who joined the Digest on his retirement in 1946, was assigned under Barclay Acheson to establish a French edition, then editions in Germany, Austria, Belgium, and Switzerland. He is now general manager of the International Editions.

The Reader's Digest today is published in 13 languages in 30 different editions for distribution in over 100 countries. It is published in various English editions for the United States, Great Britain, Canada, Australia, New Zealand, and other countries of the British Commonwealth. It is published in different French-language editions for France, Belgium, Switzerland, and Canada. The remaining editions are in Spanish, Portuguese, Swedish, Finnish, Danish, Norwegian, German, Italian, Japanese, Dutch, and Arabic.

The German edition is circulated in 58 countries, the Italian in 86, the Spanish in 71, and even the relatively small Dutch edition in 56 lands. Circulating in all the countries of Central and South America, the Spanish edition is virtually an international magazine in its own right. The two editions in Canada, one in English, the other in a French translation, edited especially for Canada in Montreal, have a combined circulation of more than 1,000,000 copies monthly.

The Digest's circulation in Western Europe—in French, German, Austrian, Italian, and Iberian Spanish—is more than 2,800,000. Nearly 1,800,000 copies in special English editions for those countries go to the Commonwealth nations of India, South Africa, Australia, New Zealand, and the British Isles. Nearly 900,000 copies circulate in Swedish, Danish, Norwegian, and Finnish. The average monthly circulation of the Japanese edition was 407,000 in 1957 and that of the edition in Arabic, 41,000. Total circulation of The Reader's Digest's International Editions, including the recently inaugurated Overseas Military Edition in English, is conservatively 8,800,000 every month—a circulation larger by millions than that of any magazine in the United States with the exception of the Digest itself.

Each of the foreign editions has in its title the words "selections from" or "the best from" The Reader's Digest or an equivalent phrase. Every article appearing in any of these editions has first appeared in a recent or past issue of the Digest in the United States; but not every article published in the parent magazine is republished abroad. Each month advance proofs of all articles in the current United States edition are sent to the foreign editors. These men and their staffs are citizens and residents of the country where the given edition has its chief circulation. They know national characteristics, sentiment, interests, customs, circumstances. These editors grade each article for its applicability and potential interest to their readers and cable their comments and decisions to Chappaqua for review and comment by the Digest editors there. The table of contents for each edition is then drawn up, and the work of translation is begun. Except for *Selecciones,* which is edited in New York, the translating is done by experts in the country where the foreign-language edition is published and distributed.

Translating is done with extreme care, not only to transfer the sense and spirit of the article accurately from one language to another, but also to render the whole in the usage peculiar to the countries where the edition will be read. As Canadian French usage is observed in Montreal, Parisian French is used in the edition for France.

Though the business offices of *Selecciones del Reader's Digest* are in Havana, the magazine is edited and translated in New York by Colombia-born Eduardo Cárdenas and a staff drawn from Central and South American countries. It was decided early that if the translating were done in any one of the Hispanic countries, it might emerge in the colloquial Spanish of that country. Result of the group translating effort in New York has been the development of a kind of written Spanish common to all of these Spanish-speaking countries in Central and South America. The Digest's stated aim in each of the International Editions is to achieve the informal style that well-educated men and women of the country use in normal conversation.

Annotated copies of the articles in English, with measurements converted and Americanisms explained, are given the translators. The finished translations are sent to groups of critics for reports on their textual accuracy and acceptability. Despite such safeguards, problems arise and slips occur. It seemed difficult, perhaps impossible, to reproduce the Broadwayese of Billy Rose in *Wine, Women, and Words,* which the Digest had condensed. Rose himself doubted that successful translation could be made. It was when the Digest got a translator familiar with both métier and argot that the job was successfully accomplished. Rose's work was translated into *Champagne, danseuses, et stylographe* by the versatile Maurice Chevalier.

The best obtainable translators for specific tasks are always used, yet once in translation "dog-eared books" became "books about dogs with long ears"—a reasonable assumption—and "a sound truck" became "a truck in good condition," also reasonable. "No punches were pulled" convinced a translator, who so informed his readers, that no blows had been struck.

In whatever language, The Reader's Digest is recognizable at a glance on newsstands around the world. The logotype, the front cover with its picture panel and listing of contents, the general format of all editions are virtually identical. All editions are the same familiar pocket size, with one slight variation. The Japanese edition is fractionally smaller. Experimentally, it was made to conform in size to the regular edition of the Digest, but the change proved impractical and the diminution was happily restored.

Except for *Selecciones,* each of the International Editions of The Reader's Digest is edited and produced abroad, employing people, plants, and services of the country in which it is issued. In this way the Digest employs about 2200 citizens in 22 different countries. The Digest has financed or helped finance great new printing presses in Cuba, Brazil, France, Britain, and Sweden. It has helped upgrade printing standards in many parts of the world. Almost all of the 2000 tons of paper consumed for the International Editions each month is produced outside of the United States. At one time the Digest was buying Norwegian paper for its Arabic edition and paying for it in New Zealand pounds. Digest printing currently is being done in Melbourne, Aylesbury in England, Montreal, Cuba, Buenos Aires, São Paulo, Stockholm, Helsinki, Copenhagen, Oslo, Paris, Essen, Vienna, Madrid, Verona, Cairo, Tokyo, and in the Netherlands. The Digest is produced as well as read around the world.

When the Digest decided to publish its two editions in Canada, it invested more than $1,000,000 in plant and equipment. An editorial, advertising, production, and subscription staff, which now numbers about 280 Canadians, were hired. Using but a single room when it started, the Digest now occupies more than 40,000 square feet in offices in Montreal and Toronto. Paper for the two editions is bought in Canada. Printing and binding of the magazines are done there. Annual manufacturing costs of The Reader's Digest run over $1,700,000. The binding of The Reader's Digest Condensed Book Club volumes which circulate in Canada is done in Canada. This instance typifies the Digest business operation abroad.

There is no Russian edition of the Digest. Communism has consistently denounced the magazine, as earlier Nazi Germany denounced it. Though thousands of copies circulate surreptitiously in communist territory, it is in the free countries of the world that the Digest is read and valued for the same reasons that it is read and valued in the United States.

Articles appearing in the domestic edition which may offend readers in another country are not republished in the edition for that country. An article on birth control, for instance, is not published in predominantly Roman Catholic countries. Sex frankness has to be watched carefully in the Arabic edition. Medical and health articles, of sure appeal in the United States and many other countries, might seem outdated to readers in modern Finland. With these exceptions, people around the world seem to respond to the same amalgam of humor, intimate biography and thrilling narrative, exposé and art-of-living material which arouses the interest of Digest readers in the United States. The Digest's nature stories, and its articles on science, travel, medicine, community improvement, and its other condensed articles on a wide variety of subjects are read as avidly abroad as at home.

Except in the Middle East, the ubiquitous and multilingual Reader's Digest has become a best-selling periodical everywhere it is published. Studies conducted by the Digest's Survey Research Department seem to show that people everywhere like much the same kind of reading material. Reader reactions show marked similarities around the world. "Life in These United States" is as popular in Japan as it is in the United States itself. "My Most Unforgettable Character" delights people in 30 editions in 13 languages in all the countries in which the languages are read. Humorous filler tickles the risibilities of the Italians, the Dutch, the Germans, the Spanish, the Japanese, and all the others as readily as it draws laughter in Ohio or Maine or Oregon. Full-length humorous articles, the surveys seem to show, seldom do well anywhere. Opinion in England, Norway, the United States, and all the other places seems to be that they are generally funniest to their authors.

At a stage in the world's history when it is pleasant to have the point confirmed, the Digest seems to have proved once again that, despite geography and climate, differences in diet, politics, morals, and speech, people everywhere are much alike. They laugh at the same things. They feel pain when they are hurt. They share a common humanity.

DeWitt Wallace attributes the favorable international reception of The Reader's Digest to the fact that his readers in many countries "like to have their mental vistas broadened and to keep abreast of the fascinating panorama of new developments in every field."

What The Reader's Digest, through its International Editions, does to create and develop international good will and understanding is impossible to estimate and might be difficult to overestimate. The Digest does more, perhaps, than most deliberate governmental propaganda or government pronouncements, always suspect, can possibly do to demolish prejudice, dispel ignorance, and through the unpretentious simplicity of condensed article, story, and humor, establish feelings of sympathy and friendship among peoples. The International Editions of The Reader's Digest are profitable commercial ventures, but they constitute also an achievement which must be measured in other than purely monetary terms.

Eve Curie said it quite simply, from the European viewpoint, in this way: "In Spanish, in Portuguese, in Swedish, in many other languages, men and women are learning what the immense, mysterious United States is really like—and learning, moreover, that many Americans have the same hopes and hungers and dreams as themselves. . . ."

CHAPTER XIX

SPECIAL EDITIONS AND SPECIAL PROJECTS

Every month during the school year nearly a half million American high-school students receive, read, and use in their studies the current edition of The Reader's Digest. The circulation, September through May, of the Educational Edition of the Digest alone is that of a best-selling magazine. It is, for instance, larger than the total circulation of *The New Yorker* and more than the combined circulations of *Harper's* and the *Atlantic Monthly*.

The School Edition, for which students pay twenty-five cents a copy, carries a 24-page Student Guide to Better Reading. The Teachers' Edition contains the student supplement and an additional 16-page Teaching Guide.

What the Educational Edition does is introduce the contemporary scene and the Digest's interpretation of it into the classroom. It supplements the teaching of the classics in English courses with informative and entertaining writing by modern writers, providing examples of stylistic excellence and skillful editing as well as literary material on subjects of interest in the world in which the student actually lives. It brings contemporaneity into history and the social studies with its discussions of the social, political, and economic problems confronting people today. The Student Guide is planned and executed—with the guidance and criticism of a long list of pedagogical experts whom the Digest retains—to help the student develop reading, writing, vocabulary, speaking, and listening skills. The stated aims of The Reader's Digest in publishing this Educational Edition are: "To encourage lifetime habits of better reading, to improve reading skills, to build thinking, informed citizens, and to help teachers do a better job of teaching."

The Educational Edition and the supplementary Digest-prepared educational texts are a completely nonprofit venture. They show no monetary return. The Digest considers the undertaking a contribution toward sound and more complete education which it makes by placing in the hands of high-school students every month its own mirror of the American and international scene. It believes that its articles of lasting interest, and its discussion of domestic and foreign problems, will provoke discussion, further understanding, and to an extent mold character.

That the Digest is in these ways of value to American education and to the individual student is confirmed by the enthusiasm with which the magazine is read and discussed in class and by the enthusiastic comments of teachers and supervisory personnel who can observe, firsthand, the improvements in reading, vocabulary, and comprehension which school use of the Digest accomplishes.

The value of the Educational Edition and its supplements to the Digest in other than monetary terms is long-range and inestimable. Though more than enlightened self-interest informs the venture, use of The Reader's Digest in the schools inculcates the magazine-reading habit, builds future magazine circulation, and spreads familiarity with and appreciation of The Reader's Digest among a highly impressionable segment of the population.

The Educational Department of The Reader's Digest also publishes 18 paper-bound books wholly for school use. All of them are composed of articles which have appeared in various issues of The Reader's Digest, but they have been rewritten on different vocabulary levels for use in the various grades. Each volume contains articles especially selected to appeal to the given age and educational-attainment group.

There are eight brightly illustrated "Reading Skill Builders" intended for use at the third, fourth, fifth, and sixth grade reading levels. There are six "Secrets of Successful Living" for English, social studies, and guidance classes from grades seven through twelve. There are two volumes of "Reader's Digest Reading." Prepared for and used by the United States Department of State in binational centers around the world and for helping literate foreigners to learn English easily, they are used also in school remedial-reading classes. Two "Adult Education Readers" are published primarily to improve reading skills among adults and for the use of adolescent students who are just learning to read English.

The Reader's Digest makes specific and generous contributions to education in still other ways. Among the stated purposes of The Reader's Digest Foundation are to help youth make the most of its capacities and opportunities, to stimulate sound Americanism, to aid research and advance in medicine, and to further religious effort on a nondenominational basis.

Under part of this plan the Digest offers a limited number of schools and university departments of journalism a modest travel expense fund for use by students in reportorial research for stories written as part of their formal course. The purpose of these grants is to encourage direct observation and to afford firsthand experience in the use of primary information sources. Students at such institutions as the Medill School of Journalism at Northwestern University and the Henry W. Grady School of Journalism of the University of Georgia have traveled and worked under these grants from The Reader's Digest Travel Expense Fund.

In 1952 The Reader's Digest Foundation established a lectureship in American literature, history, and institutions at the University of Dijon in France. The chair has been held every year since that time by some qualified teacher and scholar in American civilization, the Digest paying the professorial stipend. Plans are now under way to provide housing for the incumbent in a Digest-owned apartment during his tenure.

Currently the Foundation is engaged in a program which will expand its participation in international education. DeWitt Wallace has contributed very substantially to Macalester College, of which his father was president, on whose campus he grew up, and where he spent his first two undergraduate years. The Reader's Digest is now planning to provide funds for bringing one or two visiting foreign teachers to Macalester each year.

Besides its regular and school editions and its multilingual, multinational distribution in its many foreign editions, The Reader's Digest has wide circulation of which the general public is little aware, some of it in forms that the public seldom sees.

Since 1928 the Digest has been transcribed into Braille. Every month the American Printing House for the Blind in Louisville, Kentucky, makes and distributes 3300 cover-to-cover transcriptions which are sent free to sightless men and women throughout the United States, each Braille copy reaching about five readers. The activity is supported by the contributions of Digest readers and employees to the Reader's Digest Fund for the Blind. Sponsored by various associations abroad and also distributed gratis, Braille editions of the Digest appear also in Japanese, Swedish, Spanish, and German.

For the blind who cannot read Braille, the American Printing House for the Blind presses talking records, 1400 of each issue of the Digest, each issue requiring 12 long-playing records. These are distributed nationally through 28 libraries designated by the Library of Congress and through 72 other centers, such as homes for the blind and the aged and the various community social-service clubs.

The regular domestic edition of the Digest goes free to many thousands of men and women who could not otherwise obtain it. In 1937 the Digest announced that it would enter 1000 free subscriptions for inmates of federal and state prisons. The offer was continued in the years following. Requests which came in from other correctional and charitable institutions were likewise honored until the Digest was providing nearly 80,000 copies yearly free to these institutions. In recent years, instead of free subscriptions, unsold newsstand copies are provided for distribution. These copies given away are not included in total circulation figures for The Reader's Digest but are listed in Audit Bureau of Circulations reports as part of the Digest's "unpaid distribution."

Through a Special Services Department set up to handle this distribution, the Digest has also made its educational materials, including books developed during World War II for the Armed Services Institute to use with retarded and foreign-born readers, available to educators in correctional institutions. The editors believe that the simplified biographies, nature pieces, adventure and animal stories, which form the basic content of these books, may thus serve a purpose beyond formal education and informal entertainment. In 1955 the Digest took a further liberal step. Editors of prison papers and magazines were accorded permission to reprint Digest articles and other materials as they wished, provided only a copy of their publication be filed with the Digest for the checking of credit lines.

Other unsold newsstand copies of The Reader's Digest are distributed through service and charitable organizations to patients in state, veterans', and service hospitals, to leprosaria, to homes for the aged and needy, to youth centers, and to residents in city and county homes. As this same procedure is followed abroad with the International Editions, The Reader's Digest reaches hundreds of thousands of readers, perhaps 15 or 20 readers to the copy, in the prisons and hospitals of many countries, at sea, in the jungles, and in the dark places of foreign cities. The entertainment, inspiration, and information that the Digest places between its covers are far more widely disseminated than published paid circulation figures indicate.

In social terms this is philanthropy, characteristic Digest generosity and idealism from which its editor-publishers derive a warm satisfaction. In practical business terms these activities aid the Digest to achieve a global market saturation at all social levels which few other products and no other magazine can approximate.

CHAPTER XX

THE READER'S DIGEST CONDENSED BOOK CLUB

Ever since the first of them was introduced in the final issue of 1934, the condensed book has been a principal feature of The Reader's Digest. Thrilling adventure tales, inspirational biographies or first-person accounts, sometimes popularized discussions of serious subjects, and occasionally a novel have added depth and substance to the magazine and balanced one longer piece of writing against the variety of short articles in each issue.

Condensations of appropriate current books gave the Digest wider choice of the best contemporary writing and Digest readers a richer magazine. Both editors and readers were pleased. Readers asked for more condensed books, but this was not possible within the scope of The Reader's Digest, and there were many books, particularly good long novels, which could not be used in the magazine without throwing an issue out of proportion. It was in this way that the idea of The Reader's Digest Condensed Book Club originated.

World War II made the venture impossible. When reader pressure brought the subject sharply into focus again after the war, there were other difficulties to be overcome. Despite gratifying experiences with books condensed in the Digest itself, book publishers were dubious. It was possible that publication of condensations in bound volumes might kill the sale of new books in their complete and original form. Some authors were not convinced that their books could be shortened yet still retain their full stories, ideas, style, and flavor. The Digest foresaw other difficulties. It would be offering fiction to its nonfiction public. DeWitt Wallace would have to risk not only a large sum of money, but also the invaluable prestige of The Reader's Digest.

When in 1949 Wallace decided to go ahead with the venture, it moved rapidly. Ralph Henderson, the Digest's first editorial employee, had long been in charge of the book condensations in the magazine. Henderson, a book man, particularly a novel man, who had been instrumental in getting such novels as *The Hucksters, What Makes Sammy Run,* and *Children of God* into the Digest, was placed in charge of the operation. In one week in the fall of 1949 Henderson and A. L. Cole visited all the important New York publishers to discuss possibilities and terms. By the end of the week they were assured of the co-operation of 40 publishers. A small staff began experimenting in cutting and editing books for inclusion in proposed quarterly volumes of about 500 pages, each of which would include from three to five book condensations.

So rapidly did the plan take form and so successful did the editorial work prove that these experimental books became the actual contents of the first volume. That volume, containing *The Show Must Go On* by Elmer Rice, *The Cry and the Covenant* by Morton Thompson, *The Autobiography of Will Rogers,* and *Cry, The Beloved Country* by Alan Paton, went off in the spring of

1950 to 183,000 charter subscribers for a larger guaranteed sale than most best sellers attain.

The pattern of Reader's Digest Condensed Books was set by the first volume. Each of them now contains about 575 pages and includes condensations of four or five current books which have not been condensed in the Digest itself. The typical spring, autumn, summer, or winter volume consists of long condensations of two or more novels together with one or more shorter nonfiction condensations. The volumes are uniform in size and in the decoration of the backbones of their hard-cover bindings. Different but similar cover designs are used front and back on all volumes in the continuing series. All of the books are clearly printed in large type and illustrated in color. Full color photography was introduced in the Condensed Books in 1958.

Within a year of its founding The Reader's Digest Condensed Book Club had 512,000 members, many more than the largest book club in the United States. Within four years it had 2,500,000 members.

The Condensed Book Club follows the editorial standards and practices developed by The Reader's Digest itself, but there is a fundamental difference in emphasis. Nonfiction books are generally reserved for the magazine. Modern fiction is the heart of the Condensed Books, and those new novels which, in the opinion of the editors, have vital points to make, are informative, entertaining, and well written are chosen for the Digest volumes.

To find them the editors of Reader's Digest Condensed Books make weekly contacts with publishers in Boston, New York, and London. Working out of the Digest's New York offices, a liaison group representing the interests of both the magazine and the Condensed Book Club meets regularly with the 40 leading publishers in the city and the 20 leading literary agents to find out what books of possible Digest use will be published during the next nine months. The editors read about 2800 books a year in the United States and 1000 in England. If a forthcoming book in which they feel they may be interested is spotted on a publisher's schedule, they try to see it in manuscript form. If that is not possible, they reach it by the time the book is in first galley proofs. At least two, sometimes three, editors read it. The decision to use or reject is made at this point.

If the decision is favorable, the Digest buys the rights to condense the book, and the book is assigned to an editor for the first rough cut. Three more editors go over this first condensation, making further cuts, perhaps restoring some already made, making sure that the contents, the spirit, and the style of the author are retained in the shortened version. Nothing essential is changed. Where deletions necessitate the insertion of transitions, these are made in the manner of the author. Ralph Henderson makes the final check. The condensed book, still in Digest "manuscript," then goes to the copy desk, where a final reading is made, and the copy is prepared for the printer. The entire process takes from three to six weeks for a book which the editors may have spotted six to nine months earlier.

The Condensed Book editors believe that an author, particularly a novelist, must feel free to create his work in whatever way and at whatever length he chooses. They recognize that book publishers, for economic reasons, customarily issue books of fairly standard size to which the public has become accustomed. The editors feel that it is then their function to examine any book which offers possibilities for inclusion in a Condensed Book volume—scrutinizing it chapter by chapter, page by page, paragraph by paragraph—from the point of view, not of the critics or professional, but of the general reader. If the book is selected, they try to cut it in such a way that its total readability will be preserved and sometimes enhanced.

Condensation for brevity and time saving in reading is beside the point in the cutting of the Condensed Books. Novels, and more than 75 per cent of the books condensed are novels, have other qualities which the reader expects—pace, texture, flavor, style, as well as story. Condensing, whether of an article in The Reader's Digest or of a book for The Reader's Digest Condensed Book Club, always means that something must be omitted, but the attempt in the Condensed Books is to retain much more than the book's merely factual content. No rules govern the process. Cutting is never to an arbitrary length. The condensing of each book is a distinct and distinctly individual problem. Some books the editors, working, as do their counterparts on the magazine, for group judgment, abridge greatly. Other books, like Alan Paton's *Cry, the Beloved Country* and John Hersey's *A Single Pebble,* they have reproduced practically verbatim.

In its first years The Reader's Digest Condensed Books have brought a wide variety of novels, autobiographies, suspense stories—in each volume a content that the editors intend to make diverse, fresh, and stimulating—to a multimillion audience in this country and abroad. *The Cardinal, Blandings' Way, The Caine Mutiny, Melville Goodwin, USA, The Cruel Sea, Adventures in Two Worlds, My Cousin Rachel, The Bridge at Toko-ri, The Night of the Hunter, The Day Lincoln Was Shot, Giant, The Nun's Story, The Last Hurrah, Duveen, Elephant Bill, The FBI Story, Witness, East of Eden, The Philadelphian*—these typify the effort.

The Book Club does not consciously pick best sellers, though publication in one of its Condensed Book volumes has often turned a book into a best seller. Often, the editors say, they deliberately choose a book which because of its harsh realism or outspoken treatment of a controversial subject—*Too Late the Phalarope* and *By Love Possessed* are two examples—may disturb a proportion of their readers. On occasion, if it is one which they consider worth while for the writing or other qualities which seldom lead to best-seller status, they select a book which might go relatively unnoticed except for its condensation in a Reader's Digest book.

The authors in Reader's Digest Condensed Books run from Nobel and Pulitzer prize winners down through versatile journalists and well-known writers of light popular fiction to comparatively unknown authors who seem to have something to say and the ability to say it. The list includes Sir Winston Churchill, Henry Morton Robinson, John Gunther, A. B. Guthrie, Jr., MacKinlay Kantor, William Faulkner, James A. Michener, J. P. Marquand, Nicholas Monsarrat, Dr. Frank G. Slaughter, Whittaker Chambers, Daphne du Maurier, Irving Stone, Emily Kimbrough, John Steinbeck, A. J. Cronin, James Hilton, Pearl Buck, Dick Pearce, Alec Waugh, Viña Delmar, and John Hersey—certainly a potpourri of talents from all gradations of literary ability and performance, but most of them already big-name writers before Digest notice.

All of these writers and all of these books represent what Ralph Henderson and his associates like and believe add up to "an honest job of representing good current books." If the editors do not like a book, they do not use it, for Henderson also believes that "it is insincere editing to give the customers something you don't like yourself."

That this philosophy is correct for the job they do is attested to by the tremendous membership of The Reader's Digest Condensed Book Club. That the editors do their particular job with adequate skill is the opinion of those who might have been their most vicious critics, the authors themselves. Virtually without exception, authors whose work has been published in the Condensed Books have diplomatically written the editors expressing their pleasure, often their amazement, at the skill with which their books have been presented. The editors of Reader's Digest Condensed Books have a thick file of such letters of which they are understandably proud. These, chosen at random, are typical:

> *I have read and reread your condensation of* The Nun's Story, *with tiger-bright eyes looking for the sentences, paragraphs, or pages which perforce must be left out of any condensed version of a book. But sharply as I searched . . . I could not find just where you made your skillful cuts, so exceedingly skillful were the transitions you achieved to carry one smoothly over them. . . .*
>
> KATHRYN HULME

> *. . . I was most impressed by the way in which you had cut* Island in the Sun*—it seemed to me that you retained all the essential characters and issues—nothing of importance seemed to have been left out. It was a triumph of skillful editing. . . .*
>
> ALEC WAUGH

. . . It is astonishing that a book can be cut down so much yet retain so much of the original; an admirable piece of craftsmanship.

JOHN APPLEBY

I would like to congratulate somebody on the excellent condensation of Our Virgin Island. *If I hadn't written the book, I wouldn't have known it was condensed.*

ROBB WHITE

. . . I'm delighted by (and with) the job you've done on The Cardinal. *It's rather alarming to see how much can be cut from a story and still keep it alive . . . my congratulations on the choice of material you retained and the amount of stuff you let go. Superb!*

HENRY MORTON ROBINSON

I was astonished at the way the main plot was preserved, in about one-fifth the compass of the novel.

HERMAN WOUK

Some authors have been much more effusive in their praise. Certainly the comments of some of them are suspect. Though they were not when the Condensed Books started, authors and publishers are now paid sums ranging from $10,000 to $100,000 for Condensed reprint rights. The Reader's Digest Condensed Book Club now pays out about $1,500,000 yearly in royalties to authors and publishers. Selection by the club is tantamount to being tapped as a best seller or for a high-priced sale to Hollywood a few years ago. Yet all writers are not insincere, and the approval of those writers who are, in addition, meticulous craftsmen cannot be disputed.

When they picked *Boon Island* for the Condensed Books, editors at the Digest were warned that Kenneth Roberts, by far the finest historical novelist this country has produced and a man who took infinite pains with his facts and his writing, might prove difficult to deal with. Roberts had never before permitted reprinting of his work in cheaper than the original editions or in other than unabridged form. Roberts asked to see what cuts were made in the novel as work progressed at the Digest. The editors agreed, asking only that he co-operate on their time schedule. Roberts promised that he would. Every word of the book, which was being cut one-third of its original length, was sent to Kenneth Roberts at his home in Kennebunkport, Maine. Roberts approved them all and made no important suggestions. The only hitch was that, always the perfectionist and critical of his own work, Roberts began rewriting some of his own sentences in *Boon Island*. He stopped, very much amused, when Ralph Henderson pointed out that readers would ascribe these changes not to the author but to careless editing.

Some books have presented special problems to the Condensed Book editors. One of these, because of its length, the opacity of the style, and the unrelenting naturalism of some of its contents, was James Gould Cozzens' *By Love Possessed* in 1957. Henderson knew and admired Cozzens' earlier work. He knew that Cozzens was working on a new long novel. When he read it he found himself "overwhelmed" by the book's quality and got the novel under contract before any of the other book clubs. The contract was first an option in case the Digest editors felt they could not present the book successfully in a realistic presentation that would be fair to an honest story. The novel posed one of the most difficult editorial tasks they had assumed, but the editors produced a version acceptable to the author and themselves.

The Reader's Digest Condensed Book Club grew so fast that while the new building it occupies on the Digest grounds at Chappaqua was being constructed one wall had to be knocked down to accommodate its growth. The staff includes 15 men and women in editorial capacities and about 500 clerical workers handling subscription and other business operations. It began to go into foreign editions in 1951, and today there are Condensed Book Club editions for Canada, England, Australia, and for the French, Italians, Germans, Swedish, Dutch, and for both Spanish- and Portuguese-speaking Latin Americans. Thus the club has over one million members abroad in addition to those in the United States, necessitating readers in London and members of its business staff about the world.

In the manner of The Reader's Digest itself, the overseas volumes contain condensations drawn from a backlog of the U.S. volumes, but not necessarily the same selections appearing in the concurrent United States volume. In the United States subscribers pay $2.44, plus 12 cents postage for each volume. Beginning subscribers pay only 10 cents for the first volume. Members can cancel their subscriptions at any time. The prices of overseas editions vary, but comparable introductory offers and membership arrangements are made. Authors and publishers whose books are selected for The Reader's Digest Condensed Books are paid on an advance guarantee of 2,500,000 copies, paid later on an audited figure of actual sales, which are always above the guarantee and sometimes nearer 3,000,000.

DeWitt Wallace leaves the editorial conduct of The Reader's Digest Condensed Books largely to his experienced associates. When he does actively participate, the results are not entirely unexpected. A book which he purchased in a railway station to read on a train journey impressed him. On his return to Chappaqua he suggested in one of his familiar penciled memoranda that it be considered for inclusion in a volume of Condensed Books. The editors found that the book had been read by several staff people and that, after some debate, an adverse decision had been reached. The readers' reports were sent to Wallace, whose only reply was that he had liked the book and somehow could not forget the story. The book was re-examined, cut, and included in the next volume. It proved to be one of the most popular books with readers since the founding of The Reader's Digest Condensed Book Club.

Because imaginative literature at its best is still different from journalism, because book treatment permits of content and development not possible in the short article, Reader's Digest Condensed Books offer subjects and qualities not found in the Digest itself. In this sense the Condensed Books complement the magazine, broadening and deepening reader experience through presenting some of the best popular fiction of the day.

Americans are not a book-reading people. The United States reads pitifully fewer books than most other countries where literacy is admired and practiced. Just as it widened the total magazine audience, bringing millions to greater awareness of the contemporary scene, The Reader's Digest, through its Condensed Books, has done much to re-establish and maintain, even introduce to many, the habit of reading enjoyable books of ephemeral or lasting value.

That, according to Ralph Henderson, is what it tries to do. "We want to see more people reading good books. It means a great deal to us that our books are reaching large audiences because we ourselves greatly respect and enjoy these authors. We have that kind of missionary zeal—we want to see good books getting out. We think they are the best form of entertainment that can be had."

CHAPTER XXI

EDITORIAL RESULTS

In April 1947 The Reader's Digest ran an article titled, "Sticky Miracle in a Tube." It described the properties of a new adhesive which a New Jersey chemist had accidentally discovered. Two Newark builders tested it, acquired rights to the formula, and formed a corporation to sell it. Before appearance of the Digest article, sales ran to about $9000 a month. Two months after publication they shot up to $95,000, and the Miracle Adhesives Corporation, overwhelmed with inquiries and orders, was forced to put its assembly line on a 24-hour basis and subcontract its packaging. Its consumer sales went to well over $1,000,000 a year.

A Connecticut housewife began making homemade bread on an old stove in her garage and selling it to local grocers. Total output at first was eight loaves a day. The business grew until she was selling 25,000 loaves a week, mostly in nearby towns. After the Digest wrote up Pepperidge Farm, it became the nation's largest baker of home-style bread, doing an annual business of $15,000,000.

S. S. Pierce in Boston had been the fanciest of fancy grocers for a century when it was described in a Digest article. Orders poured into the company from around the globe. Food appeals and people wanted to sip rare teas and taste escargots or macadamia nuts. "Although I had always known that Reader's Digest reached a large audience, I was astounded at the interest created by your short article," wrote the president of the firm. "Our Boston store was deluged with inquiries from all over the world . . . additional response was felt by stores across the country that stock our foods. Even today, six years later, customers still mention the Digest article."

Paul de Kruif in "Family Doctor: Model 1955," which The Reader's Digest published in February 1955, described the qualified and competent modern family physician. He suggested that readers who wished to find such a practitioner write the American Academy of General Practice. Within a month the academy received 70,000 inquiries from college and corporation presidents, housewives, city managers, artists, and people of all kinds who had moved to a new community and wanted to locate a dependable physician to serve as their family doctor. Six months after appearance of the article, inquiries were still reaching the academy at the rate of 100 a day.

In November 1954 the Digest published an article about the Tracers Company of America, whose business is locating forgotten bank accounts, legacies, and securities. Within six months, as a direct result of the article, the company had received 438,000 pieces of mail. "Our offices are flooded with the most unbelievable assortment of old stock certificates, dog-eared, battered, crumbling, splattered with ink and other odd substances, but still readable. At least 15 per cent of those already processed have turned out to have value," wrote the president of the company.

"Sometimes I really wonder whether I should thank you for burying me under this landslide of mail."

"The Facts Behind Filter-Tip Cigarettes" by Lois Mattox Miller and James Monahan ran as a two-part article in The Reader's Digest in July and August 1957. They reported results of tests run to determine which cigarette filters were most effective in the removal of tobacco tars and nicotine. The tests showed the smoke from Kent filtered cigarettes contained the least.

Sales of Kent cigarettes immediately skyrocketed. Kent jumped into first place in sales in New York, Los Angeles, Detroit, Philadelphia, and Chicago. The Wall Street Journal reported on page one that Kent sales rose 500 per cent between May and August. P. Lorillard shares rose six points. Retail dealers everywhere were cleaned out of their stocks of the brand. Some dealers who were able to obtain new supplies sold them only to favored customers. Dorothy Thompson reported in her syndicated newspaper column that when she tried to purchase Kents at her grocer's she was told, "You won't find a carton in town. All sold out. Reader's Digest." A New York drugstore manager said, "Everybody got shook and either switched to Kents or to regular." In Louisville 1000 Lorillard workers put in 45,000 hours of overtime, and the plant's usual one-week vacation shutdown was canceled in an attempt to keep up with the demand. A sign in one supermarket told the story that applied nationally: "Sorry . . . all out of KING-SIZE KENTS blame Reader's Digest." In accordance with standard policy against retention of clients with conflicting interests, BBD&O, advertising agency serving both The Reader's Digest and the American Tobacco Company, resigned the Digest account.

When "Our Horse and Buggy Mails" by Wolfgang Langewiesche appeared in the May 1957 Digest newspapers across the country gave it news space and approving editorial comment. The article was discussed in Congressional committee, and the Postmaster General, long engaged in a running fight with American periodicals, told the United States Chamber of Commerce he believed the article served a useful purpose. Time and time again Digest articles are read approvingly into the Congressional Record.

In a typical month the Associated Press, the United Press, and International News Service will send out eight to ten stories over their wires based on facts published in The Reader's Digest and three or four hundred newspapers will run editorials on Digest articles. Governmental and business organizations, schools, and other institutions request millions of reprints yearly, giving wide additional distribution to facts and ideas published in The Reader's Digest.

Instances such as these, which could be many times multiplied, attest to the deep and widespread influence of The Reader's Digest. The Digest is read and believed, and people act upon its suggestions. Its influence is felt in government, in business, and throughout our social life. Digest articles have stimulated legislative reforms, wrought business changes, and affected the attitudes of millions toward political and social problems. The Reader's Digest is a strong force in the molding of public opinion, and it has proved that force over and over again.

The Director of the Bureau of Prisons of the U. S. Department of Justice said that the Digest, in publishing "Get the Children Out of Jail," made a direct contribution to subsequent reforms in many states. Readers have insisted that Digest articles have saved their health, their marriage, or even their lives.

A young Venezuelan paraplegic, paralyzed from the waist down, read "Where What's Left Works Wonders" in The Reader's Digest in 1949. The article described a young American lawyer, completely paralyzed from polio, who, after rehabilitation, was back at his practice in a wheel chair. Encouraged by this story of the return to active life of one whose paralysis was worse than his own, José Pirela Rust, after his release from the hospital, scraped up passage to New York. At Dr. Howard Rusk's rehabilitation center he learned to walk again. Equipped with braces and crutches, Rust returned to hospital-administration work in Caracas. In 1958 Rust was designated one of a group of some 20 Venezuelans to take advanced training in rehabilitation methods in the United States as preparation for participation in Venezuela's own rehabilitation program.

On its thirty-fifth anniversary in February 1957 congratulations came to The Reader's Digest from all parts of the world. The President of the United States wrote: "For 35 years The Reader's Digest has faithfully mirrored the character of the United States of America to increasing millions of readers . . . at a time when understanding between peoples is of inestimable importance, it has, through its international editions, mirrored the character of the United States to increasing millions of readers abroad. I congratulate you on this great contribution to the strengthening of our way of life at home and to the appreciation of that way of life by people of many lands."

Sir Winston Churchill sent his warm good wishes. The Prime Minister of Great Britain, the Chief Justice of the Supreme Court of Japan, Konrad Adenauer, Belgium's Foreign Minister, the Prime Minister of Italy, Francis Cardinal Spellman, Benjamin Fairless, the American ambassador to the United Nations, the president of the National Education Association, the commanding general of the Strategic Air Force, the president of the National Council of Churches of Christ in America, and a host of others—actors, Nobel prize-winning scientists, senators, Captain Eddie Rickenbacker, Donald Campbell—praised the Digest for its accomplishments.

The president of Columbia University said that in his opinion The Reader's Digest ". . . is doing an incalculable service wherever men are free to read." John Foster Dulles wrote: "The faith in democracy expressed in its pages has made its special contribution to world peace and freedom." Arthur Hays Sulzberger, publisher of *The New York Times,* hailed the Digest as a distinguished member of the free press: "Thirty-five years of growth and wholesome influence, both at home and abroad, have made the Digest a powerful force in our day." General Alfred M. Gruenther described himself as "an ardent Digest reader and supporter—I never miss an issue. By its interest in peace and our security, it is a powerful force for unity and security for our nation and the entire free world."

The testimony of such witnesses to the stature and influence of The Reader's Digest must be regarded as strong evidence of the magazine's unique status and unusual accomplishment, yet these opinions of leaders of church and state are not shared by everyone. The Reader's Digest is a phenomenally successful magazine, which has won the esteem and affection of millions in the United States and abroad, but it is not a monstrosity. The Digest has often been attacked for its occasional oversimplification of complex subjects, for its missionary zeal, unvarying optimism, sometimes for its article-placement policy. It is not, and has never tried to be, all things to all men. Much of its integrity and repute can be attributed to its unrelenting insistence upon being itself.

The Digest's exposés and reporting of the facts as it finds them, its stated judgments and unconcealed opinions on controversial subjects, have angered politicians on both the national and the international scene. The Digest has bitterly annoyed the chairman of the board and all the board members of more than one company, some of the more vociferous leaders of organized labor, and, often for opposite and contrary reasons, any and all pressure groups it has mentioned or, more culpably, ignored.

CHAPTER XXII

ADVERSE CRITICISM

The Reader's Digest, like most large-circulation magazines, is conservative. It believes in social and political change through orderly development. It believes in the traditions which are the heritage of the race, in religion, in the social codes which it has taken man most of his history to develop. Critical attacks on the Digest have come naturally from sources swayed by opposing philosophies.

The Digest has consistently attacked abuses of public trust. It has many times exposed bureaucratic waste and inefficiency, fraudulent or misleading advertising, misuse of its power by organized labor, and dishonest dealing, whether by nations, political parties, and highly organized minorities or by automobile mechanics, watch repairers, and real-estate dealers. The Digest has been lauded for its crusading efforts. It has likewise been vilified.

Like every medium of communication in the United States of the second half of the twentieth century, the Digest is subject to attack, often gratuitous, for failure to observe any of the taboos which have increased in geometric ratio as democracy has progressed toward its present ideal of a society without individual, social, monetary, or cultural distinctions. Minority groups, organized, affluent, and very vocal, are on the alert for slights, real or fancied, which they find equally in reference made to them or in the neglect they suffer when no mention is made.

The Digest has at various times been called anti-labor, anti-Semitic, anti-Negro, anti-Roosevelt, anti-Russian. In the same mail irate subscribers have dubbed it fascistic and communistic, pro-Catholic and anti-Catholic. Every time it publishes an article critical of some phase of the federal government's undertakings it is discovered, whichever party is in power, to be anti-administration, incorrect in its facts, and willfully wrongheaded.

In November 1942 *In Fact,* a small-circulation periodical featuring so-called "exposés," accused the Digest of fascist motives and propaganda. The *English Journal* reprinted the accusation in February 1943. A committee of the National Council of Teachers of English was appointed to investigate the charges concerning a magazine used widely in American schools. Ten months later the report was refused by the national body as making damaging charges without proof. A second report was disowned by the council and banned from publication when it met in convention in December 1944. The president of the council declared that the report "failed to examine the reliability of critics and the validity of the criticism," that it was "unscholarly . . . and full of libelous statement." The Digest was vindicated.

PM, a pro-labor tabloid of leftish tendencies, was very unhappy with the Digest for several years before the New York newspaper's demise in 1948. The Digest, according to *PM,* was always reactionary and, when *PM* was most annoyed, the Digest was a communications cartel operating like "the impersonal machine and corporate octopus" to "stifle competition and destroy competitors." *PM* had helped foment the investigation by the National Council of Teachers of English. It egged on the attack when in 1943 the Digest published an article by Hugh A. Butler, Republican senator from Nebraska.

Butler, who had visited 20 Latin-American countries, wrote that much of the $6,000,000 being spent to achieve hemispheric solidarity was being wasted and gave the reasons why. Vice-President Henry A. Wallace was horrified and apologized to all of South America for the "shocking slur." A Pennsylvania senator, Democratic, reiterated verbatim the cartel charges of *PM* and declared that the Digest had made "an international fool" of his betrayed colleague in the Senate. *PM* and sections of the Democratic party, then in power, charged the Digest with an attempt to smear the Roosevelt Administration. The Communist party in Chile organized a boycott of the Digest's Spanish-language edition. *Newsweek* reported, February 21, 1944, that "in Washington Administration circles have been flirting with the idea of an anti-trust action aimed at the Digest's policy of sewing up reprint sources with exclusive contracts."

DeWitt Wallace said simply: "We published Senator Butler's article because we believe there is too much concealment from the American people of United States Government policies in South America . . . there is evidence in many instances that the policies of the Administration may be creating more suspicion than friendship."

In July 1943 the Digest, one of the earliest of American magazines to recognize the dangers of communism, published "We Must Face the Facts About Russia" by Max Eastman. Russia was at the time a wartime ally. Eastman warned against fawning on the Soviet, saying, "To those in the Kremlin, American gullibility is only one more evidence of bourgeois decadence." Russia, he reminded Digest readers, was an absolute communist dictatorship. It was not glorifying its ally, the United States, as we were glorifying Russia at the time. "Yet this does not prevent the American communists from denouncing . . . any word spoken in honest criticism of life under the Russian dictatorship. They will so denounce the present article and The Reader's Digest for printing it." Russia was sullenly accepting American aid, at the same time denouncing American civilization in its every aspect. Stalin continually promised to overthrow imperialism, and by imperialism he meant Great Britain and the United States.

In the United States, Russia was being propagandized into sanctity in books and motion pictures. "Mission to Moscow," a film, highly favorable to Russia, made from a book of the same title written by the late ex-Ambassador Joseph E. Davies, was being extravagantly promoted and widely shown. "To me," Eastman wrote, "it is bewildering that American state officials and public champions of democracy should wish to whitewash or ignore the judicial murders, mass deportations, and state-planned famines by which Soviet totalitarianism has been established and maintained. . . ." Both communist sympathizers and those deluded by Russian protestations of friendly intent were quick to attack both Eastman and the Digest.

In December 1944 and January 1945 the Digest published "Report on the Russians" by W. L. White, a book based on a six weeks' visit to Russia. White reported factually what he saw. He described the rigid political censorship he endured. He told of high prices which made it impossible for the ordinary Russian to buy necessities, pictured the widespread poverty. He pointed out that the thrifty Soviet government ran its own black market as a state monopoly. Individual savings were viewed as a sinful sign of a tendency toward capitalism. He described deportations, the wholesale maltreatment of forced laborers, the contrasting luxuries in which the politically privileged wallowed. He saw and wrote of the vicious inequalities, the continual anti-democratic propaganda, the waste of lend-lease materials. He retailed the experiences of American technical advisers on a war project who in one month had seen 2600 of the 70,000 maltreated workers on a job die of typhus.

Though the book was favorably reviewed by the New York *Times* and even by *The New Yorker, PM* read it as a smear on Russia, the wartime ally it most admired. Labor papers attacked The Reader's Digest at the same time for a series of Louis Bromfield articles which they decided smeared labor, Franklin D. Roosevelt, and the New Deal all at the same time. This same year *The New Yorker,* which had been aware of the facts for ten years, publicly discovered the Digest's article-placement policy, objected to it in print, and refused to renew its reprint agreement. It is the only current magazine which has done this.

When the Digest ran an article on rent control, the interested *Wall Street Journal,* in an April 22, 1949, editorial titled "Coincidence Department," reprinted identical criticisms in identical language which had appeared in both the *Daily Worker,* the Communist party newspaper, and in the *C.I.O. News*. Both had written: "Never a publication to shy from giving a hearing to fascists and fascist sympathizers, The Reader's Digest February issue makes itself the vehicle for 'No Vacancies,' an antirent-control tirade by Bertrand de Jouvenel, once described in the New York *Herald Tribune* as the 'French Goebbels.'"

Such Reader's Digest articles as "How To Give Away an Air

Base," "Better Defense for Less Money," and "How Not To Handle Foreign Aid" always create wide press, radio, and television comment and usually provoke hurried defenses. "Ridiculous Waste in the Armed Services" by William L. White, in April 1955, pointed out that the Army and Navy were buying in competition rather than in co-operation and that rations were stockpiled far in advance of actual needs. The Army shipped sugar to New York to reship to Schenectady for reshipment to New York. Sailors in 1955 were eating beef, cheese, and bacon sliced in 1948. The article was immediately cried unfair by all the government agencies involved.

In April 1957 The Reader's Digest published "Our Foreign-Aid Program—a Bureaucratic Nightmare" by George Meader, Republican congressman from Michigan. The article presented detailed evidence of flagrant waste in India, Iran, Jordan, Afghanistan, and Thailand, calling these typical of hundreds of cases uncovered by investigators for the House, Senate, and General Accounting Office. Meader called for a Congressional committee equipped with funds and authority to investigate and combat waste in foreign-aid spending before the funds were spent.

Immediately the Director of the International Cooperation Administration had a long memorandum prepared, questioning the accuracy of the article. The memorandum was printed and placed in the records of the Senate Special Committee to Study the Foreign-Aid Program. Copies of the memorandum, which said that the Digest presented "a distorted picture of the total program," were also sent to members of Congress and released to the press.

For the first time The Reader's Digest broke its long-standing policy of ignoring such attacks or acknowledging them only with a general statement. The Digest, as routine, had checked all points in the Meader article. The article was rechecked after the ICA criticism, and a 14-page verification of all the facts questioned in the memorandum was issued.

The article was found to be completely correct as published. All pertinent statement had been based on public records, many of them official records of the International Cooperation Administration itself. The Digest made its research document on "Our Foreign-Aid Program—A Bureaucratic Nightmare" available to members of the House and Senate and to everyone requesting it. In an accompanying note the Digest reiterated its position: "The purpose in printing the article was not to oppose bona fide programs to help underdeveloped countries help themselves. It was to disclose to the American people what appeared by the record to be some of the evidences of waste and inefficiency which impede the use of their foreign-aid dollars."

It is comparatively easy for The Reader's Digest to refute accusations of factual inaccuracy in such fashion or to let the facts speak for themselves in such articles as "Methodism's Pink Fringe" or "Don't Be a Dupe When You Buy a House"—both of which caused shrill outcries.

It is not as easy to reply to the criticisms of some annoyed readers. In the same month one reader wrote to call the Digest "tops in modern pragmatism," though he did not say how or why; another, to say the Digest was anti-Semitic in its personnel policy, though the writer admitted in his letter that he did not know how he got the idea. An eighty-year-old reader wrote that the Digest's type was too gray, and another found a typographical error in the Braille edition. One man canceled his subscription because he did not like Arthur Godfrey; another, as a gesture of "protest against the United States action on Ruanda Urandi" (a controversy in the U.N. which the Digest had not mentioned); and a woman canceled because she felt the Digest would not like to accept money which came from stock dividends in cigarette companies.

Some reader criticism is fundamentally unanswerable. A teen-age girl wrote that "Are We Forgetting How to Walk?" was "a lousy article." An eleven-year-old reader did not believe the earth might be melted within 5,000,000 years; he believed man was good for from 5 to 10,000,000,000. Another reader was equally candid. He found an article "incredible bunk." A purist did not like the superlative form "stupidest." The father of seven children commented caustically on "Childbirth Under Hypnosis." An unsuccessful contributor of a first-person story bitterly accused the Digest of favoring professional writers over amateurs. Another reader summarized succinctly his critical impressions of the Digest: "All hogwash."

Actually few of the 10,000 reader letters the Digest gets every month are adversely critical. Many write to praise. Other readers write to ask for help or information, to exchange their opinions with the editors, or just, seemingly, to write. Every letter is answered, sometimes only with the advice that a query has been passed along to another source for more detailed answer.

School children and older students besiege the Digest, as they belabor government departments, business houses, and other magazines, with demands for term-paper material. Usually they want to know all about Crime in the United States, World History, Taxation without Representation, or whether George Washington was a greater president than Abraham Lincoln. Occasionally they get more specific:

Please send me the average weight of a fourteen-foot alligator and the number of people killed yearly by automobiles and the number killed by airplanes.

Some add pathos to persistence, as the student who ended a letter to a Digest author with, "My teacher says if you don't answer I won't pass."

An adult reader wrote simply, "I subscribe to your magazine, so I would like to apply for a job in an orchestra." The inquiry in one letter was clear and simple, "Can you tell me where I can purchase a small octopus?" A registered nurse wrote to ask the name of the "good, kind, and thoughtful person who originated the nylon nurse's uniform." She wanted to send a letter of thanks to her benefactor. Readers abroad write to ask help in emigrating to the United States or to ask cash assistance. A correspondent in Israel, who described himself as a first-class test driver and amateur mechanic, inquired about job opportunities in California. "Am I too presumptuous in seeking your advice? After all, if it were not for The Reader's Digest we would not have learned what we are missing in life, so it is somewhat your fault."

Readers often write to tell of finding copies of the Digest in odd places—in the Arctic, in the belly of a shark caught in the South Pacific—or to describe odd uses to which copies of the Digest have been put. The favorite at Chappaqua came in from the commander of a British Army Motor Transport company during World War II.

It was during the Abyssinian campaign. About four hundred miles from anywhere one of the trucks blew a gasket and we had no spares. Necessity is truly the mother of invention, and I suddenly remembered that, as always, I had a couple of

Reader's Digests in my kit. My company were natives of the Jalua tribe, who make a kind of cloth by chewing the bark of a certain tree. I called about 30 of them up and, tearing up the Digest, got them to chewing the pages. After about half an hour of hard chewing we were able to make a kind of papier-maché gasket that was good enough to take us the thousand-odd miles to Addis Ababa.

CHAPTER XXIII

TESTIMONIALS

"The Reader's Digest is both homely and sophisticated. Often as solemn as death and now and then funny as a barrel of monkeys." It was Carl Sandburg who said that. "The Reader's Digest policy of impartial treatment of major controversial problems, including labor-management relations, has gained for it a vast audience among all wage-earning groups." That was David Dubinsky. "To me the greatest thing of all about the Digest," wrote Jackie Robinson, "is that when I lay it down I am more confident about the ability of everyday people like me to make the world a better place to live in." Mary Martin found that "The Reader's Digest is more like a personal friend than an impersonal product of paper and ink . . . a friend bringing new interests, exciting discoveries, and refreshing mental experience into all our lives."

Hundreds of prominent people eminent in scores of pursuits, military, artistic, industrial, civil, and uncivil, have looked at The Reader's Digest and found it good. Their opinions, as opinions usually, reflect the characters and temperaments, the interests, insights, limitations, and perspectives of the individuals airing them. They describe the speaker sometimes more than they describe the Digest. The point which seems of significance is that each can find in the Digest what seems to him its peculiar virtues.

The president of the New York Stock Exchange found that "The Digest rounds out the economic education of millions of Americans." The president of the National Council of the Churches of Christ wrote that "The truly human insights that your articles generally reflect have found a response in millions of readers." The Secretary of State wrote: "The faith in democracy expressed in its pages has made its special contribution to world peace and freedom."

The simple state their attitude toward the Digest simply. The pretentious belabor the generalities by which they are impressed. The glib comment with journalistic facility. The salesman reads the Digest in his terms, the advertising man in his, the merchant in his.

In my opinion The Reader's Digest . . . is doing an incalculable service wherever men are free to read.

DR. GRAYSON KIRK

The Reader's Digest has been one of my favorite magazines since its first publication in 1922.

IRVING BERLIN

The gift I covet for myself I covet also for my friends: a more understanding heart, more wisdom, more restless mind. All these bounties, and good cheer, and even stern criticism

Production and distribution of The Reader's Digest is a vast and complex operation.

The paper used for one monthly issue of The Reader's Digest would form a ribbon five and one-half feet wide and 16,300 miles long. If all the copies of one issue were opened and placed side by side, it would take more than two and one-half hours for a jet plane traveling at sonic speed to traverse the issue.

Room for flower arranging at The Reader's Digest.

WANN

FORBERT

The Guest House at The Reader's Digest is a perfectly restored early-18th-century house with its own domestic staff. It is furnished with period antiques.

Distinguished visitors to The Reader's Digest and members of the staffs of the various International Editions are among those who are entertained in the Digest's Guest House.

WANN

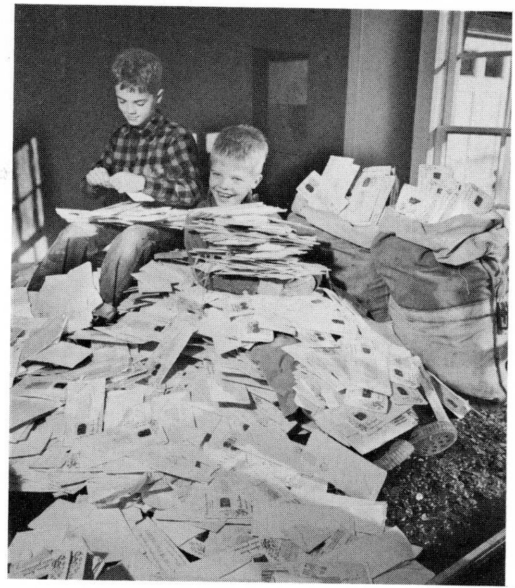

FORBERT

Members of the Mt. Kisco Boys Club retrieving pennies for use in adding to their own clubhouse. These pennies were returned after one huge direct-mail campaign for subscriptions to Reader's Digest. The Club earned half it found.

Ever since DeWitt Wallace wrote and mailed his first circulars appealing for subscriptions to his proposed periodical, The Reader's Digest has made extensive use of direct-mail campaigns to build, maintain, and increase its circulation. Mail campaigns and sampling are the basic methods which the Digest uses to attract and hold its multimillion readership. The Digest mails out more than 20,000,000 direct-mail solicitations every year, checking all mailings against its active subscription lists to avoid duplication and subscriber annoyance.

Though originally The Reader's Digest went only to subscribers, since 1929 it has also been sold nationally by single copy. Copies of the Digest, shipped through a national distribution system to magazine wholesalers and thence to retailers, are available on some 110,000 newsstands throughout the United States on the 25th day of the month preceding the cover date.

Some half million copies of the domestic edition of The Reader's Digest are printed every day on four huge Goss five-color presses at the plant of the McCall Corporation in Dayton.

All of the millions of copies of Reader's Digest Condensed Books are printed on this specially designed Levey offset press in the Sharon Hill printing plant of The Curtis Publishing Company near Philadelphia.

0,000 tons of paper a year.

Gathering and binding the Digest.

Helen Keller reading a Braille edition of The Reader's Digest. The German, Japanese, Spanish, and Swedish editions of the Digest are likewise published in Braille. The domestic edition is also transcribed on talking records for sightless men and women in the United States.

KARSH

Anthologies, compilations of articles, and a series of texts for school use, for adult education, and for language instruction are among the many and widely used books which emanate from the pages of The Reader's Digest. Every month during the school year a half million high-school students use the current edition of the Digest together with a 24-page Student Guide to Better Reading. A 16-page Teacher's Guide helps adapt the varied material to classroom use.

FORBERT

In 1958 The Reader's Digest became one of the first of the large-circulation national magazines to install a giant electronic computer for use in its subscription-fulfillment operation. Names of subscribers and addresses, together with subscription expiration dates and other pertinent data are fed into the computer, which will be able to perform efficiently and economically the enormous task of getting millions of copies of The Reader's Digest regularly and promptly to the homes of its subscribers.

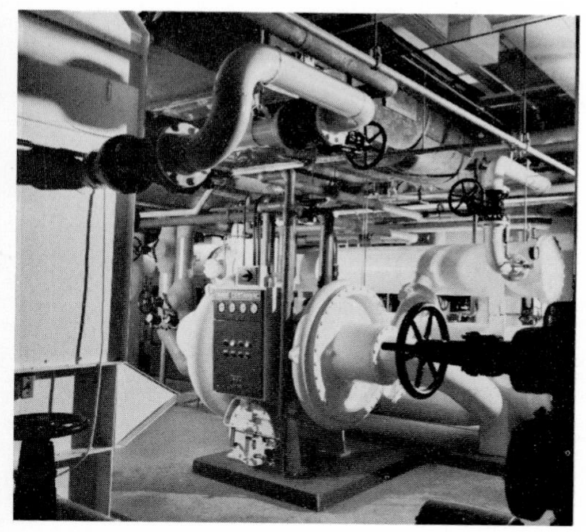

Proper functioning of the giant computer depends both on the skill of trained data processors and on complicated electrical and mechanical controls like this cooling apparatus.

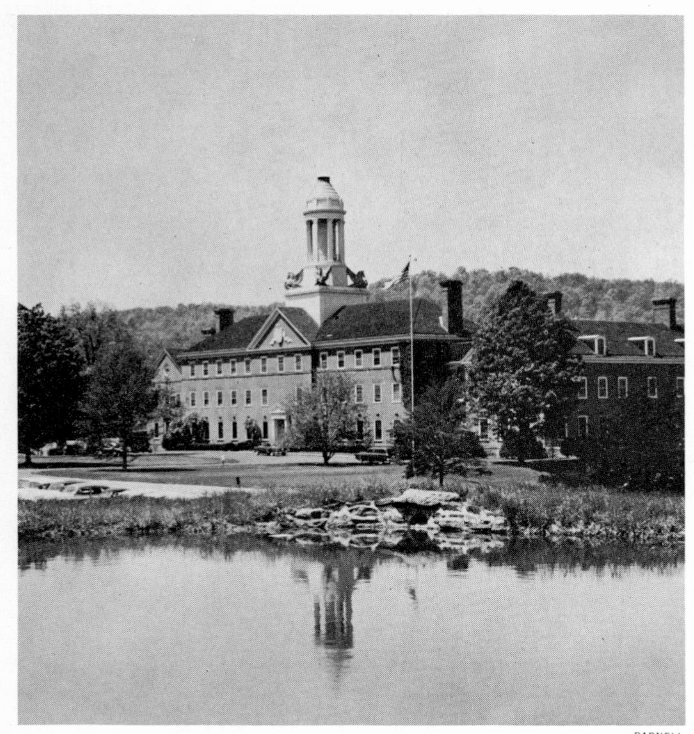
BARNELL

The white tower, with the four figures of Pegasus surrounding its base, is reflected in a pool on the grounds of The Reader's Digest in Chappaqua.

The Dragonfly Girl by Hawks forms a fountain in Digest gardens.

when needed, are combined with sheer reading delight in the pages of the Digest.

BRUCE BARTON

During the last thirty years I have read nearly every copy of The Reader's Digest.

BERNARD F. GIMBEL

Current thought is an electric thing, and Reader's Digest is one of the best conductors I know.

BENJAMIN F. FAIRLESS

Not fearing the highbrow nor scorning the popular, spicing both with gleanings of wit, The Reader's Digest has established itself as a vital part of the world we live in.

DOROTHY THOMPSON

The graduate-school dean of one of the older eastern universities: "Digest articles provide one of the most pleasant ways I know for the mathematician to supplement his symbols and the child to evolve upward from his comics"—a cogent comment. The president of the National Cash Register Company: ". . . it is an invaluable salesman for America." The Secretary of Commerce: "I am grateful that the Digest has now rounded out its service to busy readers by adding to its editorial pages an advertising cross section of the outstanding products of American enterprise." An Under Secretary of State: "Besides proving rich reading pleasure, the Digest has done more to articulate our beliefs and our way of life than any other organization I know." As part of its circulation promotion the Digest seeks out and publishes statements such as these.

Captain Eddie Rickenbacker, Samuel Goldwyn, Arthur Hays Sulzberger, Senator Harry F. Byrd, Bernard Baruch, the Duke of Windsor, Cecil B. DeMille, Paul Hoffman, Ogden Reid have all singled out the Digest as representing the ideas and ideals, viewpoints, and qualities which individually they acknowledge.

The typical issue of The Reader's Digest pulsates with an inspiring true-life narrative of man pitted against nature or his human enemies. There is another tale which will make your throat ache, then gladden your heart. Consumer reports and documented discussions of controversial subjects provide the materials for judgment. Interspersed are the quips and cranks and wanton wiles—the unforgettable characters and the slips that pass in the night. The Digest, and Carl Sandburg said this too, is "polyphonic and variegated."

"The Digest is wonderful!" stormed a very famous advertising man. (I had not contradicted him, but he never brooks the possibility.) "Something in it for everybody!"

A builder in big industrial construction, who operates his own planing mills and hardware factories on the side, paid his tribute differently. He was infuriated by the magazine's praise of a building product. Its promoters were notorious crooks. He could name a half-dozen competing products that cost less and did a far better job, but people were demanding what they had read about. "And the trouble is, everybody reads the damned Digest!"

Physicians complain that patients descend on them with complicated symptoms of new and strange diseases and demand instant cures for them every time a new De Kruif piece is published.

Convinced anew that a little medical knowledge in lay minds is a dangerous thing, these general practitioners or specialists must read the Digest to keep up with their customers.

Self-conscious intellectuals who would not touch the Digest with a ten-foot psychosis usually know the gist of every article in the last issue spurned and during the month tell me the jokes without divulging their source.

A successful novelist I know, his heart made glad with Digest money, awaited with trepidation the appearance of his latest work in a volume of Reader's Digest Condensed Books. Serious writers write the way they write because that is the way they write and usually the only way they can write. They do not like their work mangled. When the Digest volume appeared his relief neared exuberance. If his novel had to be cut the Digest had done it well.

One man had an ideal opportunity to read and ponder The Reader's Digest and reach a conclusion. Admiral Richard E. Byrd, when he lived alone for five months in the Antarctic waste, read and reread the magazine. "The six Digests I had with me seemed written exactly to fit my situation and needs. And I wager that Digest readers in a million different situations all over the world have the same feeling of a service designed with them personally in mind."

CHAPTER XXIV

ATTITUDE TOWARD ADVERTISING

The first issue of The Reader's Digest, as previously noted, carried an article which paid tribute to the contributions of advertising to human welfare. DeWitt Wallace was aware of advertising from the beginning, conscious of it as a subject of wide reader interest, and the Digest showed appreciation of advertising's virtues and accomplishments from time to time. It published many articles about advertising over the years, and perhaps twice a year it selected some advertisement outstanding for its message, design, and illustration and reprinted it with the accolade, "Advertising *cum laude.*"

The Digest was also aware of advertising excesses and abuses. Deliberately it exposed them in unequivocal attacks that struck with force, wrought some destruction, and provoked both consternation and controversy.

Twice in 1943 it lashed out at false and misleading advertising. In July, "Lifting the Cigarette Ad Smoke Screen," based on evidence brought out in actions before the Federal Trade Commission, publicized the exaggerated and unsubstantiated claims made in cigarette advertising. In August, "Taking Dentifrice Ads to the Cleaners," based on complaints against a half-dozen manufacturers in other FTC hearings, showed that there was evidence of willful misrepresentation in much of the advertising for tooth powders and pastes.

The outcries of some advertisers and advertising agencies were loud, and their complaints were bitter. The Reader's Digest was accused of unfair attacks, of using outdated case histories, of singling out specific advertisers to castigate for abuses of which many were guilty. It was accused of attempting a crusade against all advertising and, as an adless magazine, of casting doubts on the honesty of magazines which served as advertising media. It was clear to some that, through attacking advertising, The Reader's Digest sought to undermine the foundations of the American economy. There were loud demands that the Digest run a third article detailing the virtues of advertising in mass distribution and in the prosecution of the war effort.

The advertising trade press firmly approved the Digest's actions. *Printers' Ink* had long fought false advertising, the blight which caused consumers to look on all advertising with suspicion. *Advertising Age* had only praise for the Digest articles, pointing out, likewise, that all advertisers suffered from the misdeeds of a few.

This was exactly DeWitt Wallace's position. In an August 2, 1943, interview published in *Advertising Age* he said:

The simple fact is that I have as high a regard for advertising as any of those who live and work with it. I feel, however, that exposure of its abuses by a few will have a salutary effect. Exaggerated and untruthful copy hurts all advertising, and there is no excuse for it. . . . Perhaps only 2 to 3 per cent of the advertisements go to fantastic lengths in making exaggerated claims tending to tear down the credibility of all advertising. . . . It is absurd to think that "The Reader's Digest is crusading against all advertising. . . ."

One enterprising manufacturer of a popular brand of cigarettes did not complain at all. Instead the company seized on a likely bit in one of the articles, took it out of context, failed to mention the qualifications made in the article, and used it as a basis for an entire advertising campaign made to read as if the Digest recommended that cigarette. The Digest article had reported tests showing that one cigarette contained less tars and nicotine than any of six other brands tested but also said, "The differences between brands are, practically speaking, small, and no single brand is so superior to its competitors as to justify its selection on the ground that it is less harmful." The manufacturer disregarded this, headlined the impartial tests which he indicated proved his cigarette superior, and urged readers to "See what this highly respected magazine reports."

In January 1950 The Reader's Digest asked "How Harmful Are Cigarettes?" It did not actually answer the question it posed. It did suggest that mild smoking, perhaps six cigarettes a day, did the normal person no apparent harm. The article reported that a cigarette used in a holder to filter the cigarette being smoked removed 70 per cent of the nicotine and use of a silica-gel filter about 60 per cent. It did not mention paper filters of any kind. Yet the manufacturer of a cigarette with a paper filter tip hailed the article as an endorsement for his brand: "Read January Reader's Digest To Find Out Why Filtered Cigarette Smoke Is Better for Your Health—you will want to switch to the cigarette which filters your smoke."

In another of its reports to consumers the Digest published "New Brush-off for Dental Decay." The article, condensed from *Better Homes and Gardens,* examined the pretensions of what were then the new ammoniated tooth pastes and powders. Basing its facts on the findings of a two-year study at the Dental School of Northwestern University, the article stated that tooth decay was caused chiefly by the presence of sugar in the mouth. It recommended brushing the teeth morning and night and rinsing with water after every meal as a useful agent in the prevention of cavities. Practically every manufacturer of dentifrices, of mouthwashes, and of toothbrushes somehow discovered that the Digest had declared in his favor and said so loudly and at length in his advertising.

There was flattery in the fact that all these advertisers held up the unassailable Digest name as a guarantee of their own veracity and the excellence of their products, but it was not the kind of flattery The Reader's Digest could accept or comfortably wear.

The magazine was forced to warn the public against being deceived by unauthorized use of its name by advertisers. It did not grant permission to advertisers to use quotations from its articles, but it could not legally prohibit an advertiser from referring to a statement provided the reference was not literally false. In October 1950 its statement read: "The phraseology and layout of certain advertisements have misled readers into believing that the Digest has endorsed the product being advertised. In other instances by taking statements out of context an appearance of Digest approval has sometimes been obtained even when the whole tenor of the article was thereby falsified."

Despite these statements, the distorted advertising continued. The Digest repeated its disclaimers in November. In December

1950 it ran an editorial, "About Those Advertisers." Despite repeated warnings, the editorial stated, "Some advertisers have continued to misuse the name of the Digest in their advertising. Hence, our readers are again cautioned to appraise with skepticism advertisements—in the press or on the air—of trade-named products which imply RD endorsements. . . . To purchase such products on the basis of a semblance of Digest support for claims made in the advertising is to lay oneself open to the possibility of deception."

The Reader's Digest impinged on advertising in still another way. Products favorably mentioned in its reports sprang into instant favor. Time after time favorable mention in the Digest has led to a product's being swept from the open market by a stampede of purchasers.

In 1946 the Digest published "Water Stay Away from My Door." The article, condensed from *Forbes Magazine,* brought a product for waterproofing cellars to favorable notice. The product had been rated as "excellent" by the U. S. Bureau of Standards. Within a month the manufacturers had received 50,000 letters, postcards, and telegrams containing orders, requests from dealers to handle local distribution. A Brooklyn department store featured a reproduction of the Digest article in large-space newspaper advertisements. Jordan Marsh in Boston immediately sold out its supplies. Controversy as well as booming sales resulted when the Bureau of Standards disputed some of the claims made for the product.

The Reader's Digest lauded a rug cleaner, and its sales skyrocketed from $321,666 to over $10,000,000 the next year. In February 1953 the Digest published "They Make Tough Meat Tender," an enthusiastic article on a meat tenderizer. Available supplies of the product were swiftly exhausted. For six months the manufacturer received an average of 10,000 letters a day resulting from the Digest article, a total of over 2,000,000 inquiries within six months. Wire orders came in at the rate of 250 a day, so many that Western Union requested the company to install a direct wire. Manufacturing which had been confined to one plant had to be extended to six plants.

In reverse, a Digest article of January 1951, titled "Those Million-Dollar Aspirins," attacked nine patent drug products for sensational and unscrupulous advertising. It named the branded products which it described as "wonder drugs that are supposed to loosen crippled joints, reduce swelling, and stop the excruciating pains of arthritis and other rheumatic diseases." The only medically active ingredient in most of them, the article stated, was aspirin. The manufacturer of one of the products named sued the Digest for libel and lost.

The Digest published consumer reports on laxatives, toys, automobile anti-freezes, and other products, reports mostly concerned with the products of whole industries. When it believed a brand inferior it said so. When it believed a brand superior it said it was superior. It found duPont Orlon good and announced its finding. It tested a branded car wax, found that it preserved the paint and maintained the car's new appearance, as its manufacturers claimed, and so reported. Some advertisers pointed the finger of suspicion at what they insinuated was disguised publicity.

This was part of the background when, after 33 years of publication, The Reader's Digest announced in 1954 that, for the first time, it would admit advertising to its pages.

CHAPTER XXV

ACCEPTANCE OF ADVERTISING

The Reader's Digest did not come easily or quickly to the decision to publish advertising. The Digest had established itself entirely through its editorial content and was proud of the achievement. The absence of advertising was almost part of the Digest trade-mark. Some readers viewed it virtually as a guarantee of the magazine's courage and impartiality. There were other vital considerations. Would the other magazines continue to sell reprint rights to the Digest if it became a competitor as an advertising medium?

Answers were sought to some of these questions, and to one, at least, the reply was definite. In 1947, faced with the necessity of readjusting the business policy of its Canadian edition, the Digest surveyed readers in Canada to find out whether they would prefer a Reader's Digest with advertising or one without advertising but the price raised to thirty-five cents a copy. Results of the survey showed that 80 per cent preferred to see the Digest take advertising in Canada. In July 1954 a similar survey was conducted in the United States. A national cross section of Digest readers was questioned in personal interviews. The interviewers left a masked copy of the Canadian edition containing advertising and a copy of the United States edition which carried none. The next day they returned and asked whether the readers preferred the edition with advertising or the one without it at a price of thirty-five cents a copy. The percentage in favor of advertising was slightly higher than in Canada, 81 per cent.

Still The Reader's Digest hesitated to break with its own tradition. The possible change was discussed and debated for months by the Digest's owners, top editors, and business executives. However they argued and from whatever viewpoints they looked, they were faced with economic facts that stubbornly refused to disappear. Between 1939 and 1954 paper and printing costs had risen just 170 per cent. Digest editorial costs, always high, were mounting higher each year. The other costs of publication had risen at a comparable ratio, and they were still rising. The price of The Reader's Digest was still what it had always been, $3 for a year's subscription, twenty-five cents a single copy. Victimized by its own success and the inflation which followed World War II, the Digest was in difficulty. Though every other undertaking of the Reader's Digest Association was showing a profit, A. L. Cole reported to DeWitt Wallace that the Digest itself was facing a deficit of over $1,000,000 for 1954.

The decision was made one November afternoon in 1954, and an announcement was prepared which simply and clearly stated the facts:

> *Although the Digest circulation is the largest in history—over 10,000,000 copies in the United States alone—costs have now reached a point where a deficit in the magazine's operations is faced unless new revenue is found.*

Almost everything else has risen in price. The Digest still sells for 25 cents, as it did 33 years ago—when it contained only about one-third as many pages as at present.

Polls of readers indicate an overwhelming preference for inclusion of advertising rather than an increase in the price of the magazine. Starting with the April '55 issue, therefore, a limited amount of the highest grade advertising will be accepted. For at least one year not more than 32 pages of advertising will appear in any issue. There will be no alcoholic-beverage, tobacco, or medical-remedy advertisements. The advertising should be of unusually high reader interest.

There will be no reduction in the number of editorial pages, and the budget for editorial material and new talent will continue to be increased from year to year. Under the new program it will be possible to give readers more for their money than ever before.

Release of the announcement was delayed.

"Well," Wallace told A. L. Cole, "if we are going to do this thing, I suppose we ought to let the other publishers know about it first."

"That settles it then?"

"If you still think it is what we should do."

Cole hurried to the telephone. On the way he broke the news to Fred Thompson, Jr., now advertising director of the Digest.

Thompson hurried to New York, seized a startled copy chief at the J. Walter Thompson advertising agency, and together they began work on an advertisement announcing the Digest's decision. They worked on it most of the night and all that weekend, had it set in type secretly on Sunday afternoon in a job printing shop in Bridgeport, Connecticut.

The advertisement never ran. By the time it had been read and approved, the news was out in the advertising and publishing world and orders were already pouring in. One New York advertising agency executive rushed through an order for 12 full-color pages. A little later he called back to ask, "By the way, what's the price on that?" The price then was $31,000 for a full-color page, one insert. The price for a two-color page was $25,500; for black and white, $26,500—the highest rates ever charged by any American magazine but, because of the Digest's great circulation, low on the basis of cost per page per thousand subscribers or newsstand buyers who would see and read an advertiser's message.

Another advertising agency head tried and tried to reach the busy Cole. Finally he left a message: "If you won't come to me, I'll come to you. Just tell me where."

Cole and Thompson met him in New York for a five o'clock appointment. He was surrounded by other agency executives. "You the advertising manager?" he demanded of Thompson. "Then I guess you get these." He handed Thompson a thick stack of orders. The new advertising manager read only the top few—an order for 24 pages for an insurance company, another for 24 pages for a food advertiser, an order for 12 pages . . .

The Digest made it clear that it would continue to publish its consumer reports and other articles in which products were mentioned favorably or unfavorably. It would not permit use of the Digest name in advertiser's copy. It would reject all advertising it judged unsuitable. Nothing acted as a deterrent.

Within two weeks the Digest had received orders for 1,107

pages of advertising, more than three times the number it could accept for the entire first year. Before any issue of the Digest containing advertising appeared 11 million dollars in space had been placed.

The Reader's Digest had to apportion its available space among 60 advertising agencies representing 170 products and services. It selected its advertising for the first year on the basis of the space requested by each advertiser, by diversified advertising classifications so that each major category would be represented, by the past records of applicants in magazine advertising, and by the desires of those advertisers who had been consistent users of advertising space in the Digest's International Editions.

When the April 1955 issue of The Reader's Digest appeared it contained 216 pages instead of the previous 168. Full-color advertisements on glossy paper made it a thicker and far more colorful magazine. The list of advertisers represented read like a blue book of American business and industry. They were listed with awe in the press, as though their admission to the Digest was a distinction of which they could be proud.

Undoubtedly they were, but they had bought the Digest for what they considered sound business reasons. For years advertisers had looked covetously on The Reader's Digest, hoping it would open its pages to advertising. Many had urged it long since. The great and growing Digest circulation, the proved and demonstrable faith which readers have in the magazine, made it seem a valuable and unusual advertising medium. Agencies and advertisers had grasped avidly at the opportunity of reaching the world's largest magazine market with their sales messages.

No magazine withdrew from the Digest its permission to condense and reprint selected articles. Many publishers saw the Digest's move as an aid in achieving magazine solidarity against the competing medium of television. Advertising in the Digest would extend the influence of all magazine advertising.

The halcyon but unnatural situation of advertisers besieging The Reader's Digest to accept their copy and their money did not last long. The Digest's limited number of advertising pages could not supply white space for all who wished to buy, fit the frequency and continuity plans of others, or allow the manipulation of schedules in accord with the seasonal patterns of still other advertisers. After the initial enthusiasm had spent itself, the research units of agencies and advertisers began to study the results and forecast the potentials of Digest advertising, just as they scrutinize these in other advertising media, and commitments were delayed, pending the results of these studies.

When Digest advertising revenue began to fall off, due largely to the magazine's self-imposed restrictions, it was forced to change from limiting advertising to 32 pages to allowing 20 per cent of the pages in each issue for advertising purposes. This more flexible arrangement allowed advertisers and agencies space as needed and greater ease of scheduling. The proportion of advertising to editorial content is still low in the Digest, less than half what it is in most mass magazines, where the average is 47 per cent advertising to 53 per cent editorial.

The Digest, of necessity, established an advertising staff. Its main offices are in New York, where the managerial, promotional, sales, and survey-research activities are centered. Branch advertising sales offices were established in Detroit, Chicago, and Los Angeles. Large sums were appropriated for reader research to substantiate the Digest's advertising claims.

The Reader's Digest was no innocent venturing into fierce

competition in a rough and tumble arena when it went into advertising in 1955. It had already had fifteen years of sound advertising experience with its International Editions. In accepting advertising for the United States edition it was following the same pattern it had established with its first Spanish-language edition in 1940. Advertising in *Selecciones del Reader's Digest* had first been restricted to 32 pages open to a selected list of companies in the United States doing an international business, then expanded as the medium proved its value and advertisers demanded more space.

By 1946 the French edition carried up to 70 pages of advertising with a large volume of four-color advertisements, and there were 132 advertisers using at least three pages a year in one or more of the five international editions then published. Most of them were large American corporations, such as Eastman Kodak, Gillette, International Harvester, Socony Vacuum, Standard Oil of New Jersey, U. S. Steel, Texaco, Lockheed, and Swift. The Timken Roller Bearing Company was the first to use the complete list of the International Editions of the Digest in 1953, placing, through Batten, Barton, Durstine & Osborn, six full-page insertions on an every-other-month schedule, using two colors in all editions except the Canadian, which was kept to black and white.

In 1954 the 29 international editions of The Reader's Digest carried more than 15,000 pages of advertising for more than 2000 different advertisers who were investing about $13,500,000 for the year. Advertising, limited in all editions, took up about 30 per cent of their pages.

In the last three quarters of 1955 the American edition of The Reader's Digest grossed $8,000,000 from the sale of advertising space. In 1956, with the 32-page rule in effect for half the year, it grossed almost $12,000,000. In 1957, its first full year of normal operation, the Digest's gross income from advertising neared $18,000,000.

Many advertisers were quickly and thoroughly convinced of the efficacy of their advertising in The Reader's Digest. Food, appliance, insurance, building materials, and advertisers in almost every category have been pleased at the impact of their advertisements in the Digest and quoted figures to prove the results directly traceable to them.

One insurance company credited its Digest advertising with obtaining 750,000 new customers and a business increase of $25,000,000 within a year. A manufacturer of home heating and air-conditioning equipment called his Digest advertisement in 1956 "by all calculations the most successful we ever published." A food-product advertiser credited an advertisement in the Digest with a 30 per cent increase in sales in one month, writing, ". . . in every territory—and virtually in every store—hundreds of thousands of people who had read the ad . . . quietly went to their stores, and if they found the product, they quietly bought it and liked it."

In February 1956 the Weyerhaeuser Timber Company ran an eight-page, full-color advertisement in The Reader's Digest as a report to the public on the conservation and management of privately owned timberlands. The newspapers picked up the story. Complimentary letters poured in to the Digest, to the Weyerhaeuser Company, to the American Forest Products Industries. Some 60,000 reprints were requested and distributed by the National Education Association, the Izaak Walton League, the U. S. Forest Service, and other interested groups. The Digest itself got hundreds of letters lauding the advertisement from government departments, college presidents (62 of them) and deans, and from business executives. Many of these requested reprints, and there were 272 requests for films on the subject directly attributable to the advertisement. The complete advertisement, and it is unusual for any advertisement, was read into the *Congressional Record* and later reprinted in *Forestry Digest*.

The Digest's carefully preserved file of advertising success stories grows with every issue. So does another file of reader letters containing the pleased exclamations—many of them naïve, but obviously sincere—over the advertising they see in The Reader's Digest. The Digest knew that the circulations of its English and Canadian editions had expanded at a more rapid rate after they began to publish advertising than before. It had not been too sure of reader reception when it began to take advertising in the United States. In fact, it had expected some subscription cancellations and fall off in newsstand sales. They did not occur. Not only did the circulation of the United States edition continue to climb after advertising was accepted, but also readers immediately expressed their pleasure in the larger and more colorful issues.

The simple fact seems to be that most Americans like advertising. They expect to find it in their magazines. They read it as news. They are conscious of advertising and look to it for excitement and novelty in copy and display. Often the advertising provides as much information and entertainment as some of the editorial matter, and always it is an accurate running commentary on day-to-day life. When The Reader's Digest began to take advertising in 1955 it added to its value as a complete magazine.

CHAPTER XXVI

CIRCULATION SALES

When in Pittsburgh in 1921 DeWitt Wallace wrote his first promotional letters for the still nonexistent Reader's Digest, he set the selling pattern for his magazine, as he had already set its editorial pattern. Unable to interest magazine publishers in his proposed periodical, he went straight to the public through direct mail. Ever since, the Digest has based its strongest selling effort on direct-mail appeals. The Digest is one of the largest users of direct-mail advertising in the United States, and DeWitt Wallace is, indisputably, one of the country's most successful direct-mail salesmen.

As soon as the first of them were available, Wallace printed as filler in the Digest and as central text in his direct-mail advertising the favorable testimonials of pleased readers. Testimonial advertising is still basic with the Digest. One of the oldest devices in advertising, the honest testimonial is still one of the most effective. The Reader's Digest uses two types, testimonials from celebrities and testimonials from unsung, uncelebrated ordinary men and women.

Testimonials from the well-known are influential simply because they come from those whose names and achievements are familiar to most people. If The Reader's Digest is good enough for Presidents and prime ministers, actresses, Nobel prize winners, famous athletes, university and corporation heads, successful writers, generals, admirals, the reader is apt to think that the Digest may also be good enough for him. Testimonials from people who, he feels, are much like himself—teachers, doctors, lawyers, salesmen, mechanics, housewives—may not compel as much attention, but they are almost as effective. A reader feels that he is in the comfortable company of his peers. He is not overstepping himself by wanting what was not intended for him. He is just asking for what others, no better and no worse than he, have found useful and pleasant.

The other very effective sales device which The Reader's Digest has used successfully from the very beginning is sampling. Sampling is another old and tested selling method and, pragmatically, one of the soundest. It works—if the product proves good. All the subscriptions DeWitt Wallace sought and received from charter subscribers to the Digest were provisional. They were contingent upon his producing the kind of magazine those subscribers hoped and thought The Reader's Digest would be. Trial subscriptions could be canceled without any obligation if those first readers were not satisfied with the magazine when it appeared. Later subscription appeals were made under the same agreement. The subscriber could cancel at any time after receiving the first copy, with no questions asked and no monetary loss.

In effect, the Digest still uses sampling as the basis of its subscription sales operation. Short-term subscriptions and combination offers are the sampling procedure the Digest uses to introduce the magazine to new readers. Its circulation staff know from long and thoroughly tested experience that many short-term subscribers will renew on a regular basis and that many of them will keep on renewing year after year. The subscription renewal rate of the Digest, one of the best evidences of reader faith, has always been high. It runs now well over 70 per cent. Out of every 1000 new subscriptions the Digest receives, some will still be active 19 years later.

Every Christmas season finds the Digest deluged with subscriptions. From its earliest years Wallace has promoted this with special offers, and the Digest's Christmas business has always been good. In most years more than 2,000,000 people receive a subscription to The Reader's Digest as a gift. At the same time about 1,000,000 donors enter their own new or renewal subscriptions. Most of the gift subscriptions are renewed year after year, and many recipients of gift subscriptions become donors in their turn, giving gift subscriptions to the Digest to their friends.

In the early years of the Digest every dollar which could be spared was invested in direct-mail solicitation for subscribers. As more money came in more was expended, and Digest circulation mounted as a result. "It takes a long time," DeWitt Wallace remarked musingly not long ago, "before you can put a million dollars into one mailing." The Digest has done just that many times. Direct-mail selling accounts for nearly 80 per cent of the magazine's subscriptions. The Digest now mails out more than 20,000,000 direct-mail pieces annually, reaching practically every listed telephone subscriber in the United States. All mailings are checked against the active subscription list before they are sent to avoid duplication and unnecessary annoyance. This is an expensive operation, but it is Digest selling policy to keep subscriber annoyance at as low a level as possible.

As a device to attract attention in one huge direct-mail campaign in 1957, the Digest enclosed two pennies visible through the transparent panel of an envelope. It went first to the United States Mint with a request for a needed 40,000,000 pennies. The Mint refused, explaining that to supply them would disrupt the supply of pennies in circulation. Unable to obtain this many pennies from the banks, the Digest went to a New York firm which recovers pennies from vending machines, washes them, wraps them, and supplies them to banks. The Digest mailed out these 40,000,000 pennies in a very successful campaign—and, incidentally, did disrupt the penny supply. The Mint now offered the magazine all the additional pennies it might require, explaining that by circulating nationally pennies which ordinarily would have re-entered circulation in the New York area, the Digest had already caused more trouble than if the Mint had provided them in the first place.

Inevitably in a mailing of this size some pieces are returned as undeliverable. In another exhibition of the wise use of generosity which has characterized Digest business and editorial operations since the beginning, the magazine arranged with the Mt. Kisco Boys' Club to extract the pennies from the returned envelopes on the basis of a penny for the Digest, a penny for the club. The Boys' Club earned $15,000, and the Digest got a time-consuming task performed.

In addition to direct mail and solicitation through forms printed or inserted in the magazine, the Digest uses what it calls community representatives to obtain subscriptions. A note in the magazine in 1926 suggested that subscribers earn money by becoming part-time sales representatives. There are now some 40,000 of these Digest subscription salesmen, among them two who responded to the original suggestion in 1926 and 8000 who have been doing this work for more than 20 years. A typical representative—teacher, fireman, salesman, accountant, farmer, librarian, secretary, hotel manager, insurance man, mechanic, or retired man or woman—writes 20 subscriptions a year. A few of them write several thousand.

The unique feature of the Digest's subscription operation is that the magazine has always been sold either direct-mail or through these amateur, part-time salesmen. The Digest has no subscription field staff. It has no telephone operatives. It uses no subscription agencies, though a few catalogue agencies are retained as a service to people who wish to subscribe to a group of magazines through a single source. The Digest has no traveling subscription crews, employs no "crips and gimps," inelegant phrase used by the trade to describe the inelegant and often illegitimate tactics of some magazine subscription effort.

At last A.B.C. count the total United States circulation of The Reader's Digest exceeded 12,000,000. Of this number more than 9,000,000 were subscription sales. In October 1957 the cover price of the Digest was advanced from 25 to 35 cents. Instead of the usual fall off expected in such circumstances, the newsstand sales increased 100,000 for the month and single-copy sales of the Digest reached 2,218,600 at that time. Current circulation of The Reader's Digest, both subscription and single-copy, is ahead of the latest official count.

Single-copy sales are in themselves a valuable segment of the Digest's total circulation. They indicate spontaneous consumer demand and are evidence to advertisers of the magazine's issue-by-issue vitality. The Digest has the largest newsstand sale of any monthly magazine, a promotional advantage. Single-copy circulation is of additional importance as perhaps the best kind of sampling the magazine can obtain.

The Reader's Digest, distributed through S-M News, is available simultaneously on about 110,000 newsstands throughout the country on the twenty-fifth day of the month preceding the cover date. Traditional outlets for single-copy magazine sales are actual newsstands in newspaper and magazine stores, in railroad stations, hotel lobbies, and similar places. The drugstore equipped with completely stocked racks is a standard magazine outlet. With the development of the shopping center and the idea of one-stop shopping, the supermarket has become a major new and coveted magazine outlet.

The newsstand selling of magazines is a complicated and difficult business. A magazine must have the services of one of the large national distributors to get its copies to the wholesalers in an area, thus to the retailers. The wholesalers and retailers handle hundreds of competing magazines. A given title can easily be lost or disregarded in the confusion of shipment and reshipment. Enough copies of the magazine must reach the consumer outlet so that there will be a small percentage of returns. There must be some returns as assurance that the outlet has been saturated—that there were enough copies to supply those who wished to buy.

There can be little active selling of magazines single-copy. The dealer does not hawk a selected title; his selling effort ends with simply stocking it. Sales depend on the advance publicity given an issue through local newspaper and poster advertising, on the availability of copies, and on the display given the copies so that they serve in themselves as reminder advertising and stimuli to impulse purchase.

Competition for advantage is severe along the entire line of distribution. It is particularly severe in the striving for display space. Magazine publishers devise and install special racks, which the dealer uses, neglects, or in which he decides to insert competing magazines or non-magazine notions which he also sells. Rack installation and use must be checked constantly by representatives of each national distributing system. Obviously every magazine cannot have preferential display. Competition for at least equal display is continual. Swollen logotypes, vivid covers banded with even more vivid announcements of features inside the covers are all part of it. That a dealer has the Digest in sight on Monday does not mean it will be visible on Tuesday. Some dealers operate on the theory that the best-selling magazines need no display. They can be kept out of sight because customers will ask for them. These are the kinds of problems which must be met and solved continually in the newsstand selling of magazines.

The Reader's Digest has devised its own methods of solving some of the most important of these problems. During the first ten days of the on-sale period of an issue the Digest runs twenty 40-line advertisements in the newspapers of the larger cities, each of these advertisements listing and describing the contents of the features in an issue. The Digest spends $1,000,000 a year in this kind of advertising.

The Digest, because of its smaller size, was dwarfed in flat counter display by the other large-selling magazines such as *Life, Look, The Saturday Evening Post, Ladies' Home Journal, McCall's,* and *Better Homes and Gardens.* A. L. Cole reasoned that four stacks of the Digest would give it area and display equal to that of the magazines of quadruple dimensions. When distributors objected that this was a flagrantly unfair and completely unenforceable demand, the Digest arranged 100 displays of the proposed kind in retail outlets, paying for them in Reader's Digest Condensed Book Club memberships to the co-operating dealers. Sales in the test outlets went up an average of 30 per cent.

A campaign was then instituted to make this four-stack display general. Dealers selling under 50 copies monthly were offered a Book Club membership for participation. Those selling more than 50 copies were given a cent and one half additional on all copies over that number for four-stack display. As a result, many leading magazine outlets now have four-stack displays of The Reader's Digest. Between 10,000 and 15,000 such displays have been installed and are being maintained.

A. L. Cole turned his attention to the supermarkets. In 1956 supermarkets sold only a fractional amount of the Digest's total single-copy sales. Many supermarket chains and operators refused to sell magazines because they would not allocate valuable floor space to large racks displaying a distributor's entire line of all the popular magazines together with a long list of sensational periodicals, comics, and pulps. The Digest had distribution in only 8000 supermarkets, while *TV Guide* was sold in racks at the checkout counters in 22,000.

To test the possibilities, copies of the Digest were placed at supermarket checkout counters in various chains in several large cities. Sales at the various points leaped 100, 500, and even 1000 per cent. Agreements covering checkout counter displays of The Reader's Digest have now been made with some of the largest chains, and others are in process. The Digest has such displays in 3000 Atlantic & Pacific stores, each of which has about 10 checkout points. Similar agreements are being effected with Penn Fruit, Food Fair, and other large supermarket chains.

Only one thing makes possible the success of both the Digest's subscription and single-copy sales efforts, its editorial content and quality. An unwanted product cannot be advertised into commercial success. The Reader's Digest pleases the public for whom it is intended.

For many years the true circulation of The Reader's Digest was a closely guarded secret. DeWitt Wallace knew that if it became known a spate of imitators might be expected. There were already many. Though he stopped collecting them some years ago, Wallace has behind a sliding panel in his Chappaqua office a shelf of more than 200 different publications in many languages, all of which aped the Digest in size and format, even to type style and imitations of the Digest logotype, and almost all of which are now nonexistent. Wallace feared, too, as he had when considering placing the Digest on the newsstands in 1929, that if the size of his circulation were known, the publishers of other magazines from which he drew material might look upon the Digest as a dangerous competitor and cancel reprint rights.

As it did not run advertising, the Digest was under no obligation to declare its circulation. There were guesses, but the Digest issued no statements. The first announcement of actual figures was made by *Fortune* in its 1936 article which drew the attention of a surprised public to the actual size of "the little magazine" by that time.

When the newspapers or the trade press could obtain actual figures later for the circulation of the Digest's International Editions or reliable estimates of its domestic circulation, they published them as important disclosures. The Digest, as it continued to grow, consistently underestimated the size of its circulation. It piqued curiosity by veiled admissions. For a time it ran a line at the bottom of the front cover admitting that circulation was "over 4,000,000," later, "over 8,000,000."

The New York Times, September 8, 1953, crediting its information to an advance issue of *Tide* for October, broke the news: "For the first time in thirty-two years The Reader's Digest has given figures for its circulation in the United States and Canada. . . ." The figures released by the Digest were, at that time, 10,484,065 for the domestic edition and 869,769 for the two Canadian editions, a total of 11,353,834. The Digest was then going to one out of every four families in the United States and Canada.

When The Reader's Digest began to solicit advertising in 1955 it gave its United States average net paid circulation as "in excess of 10,000,000 copies per issue." It was necessary now for the Digest to give an accurate accounting of its circulation to advertisers and advertising agencies so that they would know the size of the audience they could expect to reach through purchase of advertising space in the Digest.

Until 1914 newspapers and magazines announced what circulation figures they pleased. These were published in their own statements and duly recorded in Rowell's, later Ayer's, Directory and other trade references. The figures, which could not be checked, were seldom conservative. Often they were gross exaggerations. In 1914 the Audit Bureau of Circulations was formed to provide verified totals by outside accountants of the actual circulations of member newspapers and magazines. Most of the important periodicals of the United States are A.B.C. members.

The first A.B.C. count of the circulation of The Reader's Digest was made for the January–June period of 1955. The audit, the largest ever done, showed that Digest circulation, excluding bulk, stood then at 10,098,849. Because the move necessitated large-scale clerical change in its normal subscription fulfillment operation, the audit cost The Reader's Digest about $500,000. The Digest then proposed a new, more efficient, and far less costly system to the Audit Bureau. The proposal, under study by A.B.C. management for 18 months, was tested and unanimously approved by its board of directors. It is now being used to arrive at an exact count of the circulation of The Reader's Digest.

The new auditing system, based on random sampling techniques, involves the selection of a 1 per cent sampling of subscription orders to obtain a verification of total paid circulation. This is essentially the same statistical sampling technique used widely throughout industry and in statistical research. The change is considered by the publishing industry to be an important advance in circulation-measurement techniques. It is expected that the new methods will be widely adopted by other publishers of large-circulation periodicals, with consequent simplification of labor and saving of money.

Since World War II competition among magazines in the sale of advertising space has resulted in the devising of ingenious ways of measuring the total audience of a periodical rather than simply counting the noses of subscribers and newsstand buyers. Various studies have been made by various research organizations which have attempted to measure total readership. These have resulted in the multiplication of audience figures through the counting of secondary as well as primary readers, readers in the family, pass-along readership after the copy has been read by the original purchaser and his family group and been given to others, the multiple readership in such places as doctors' and dentists' offices and the like. Huge figures have become commonplace through the efforts of the magazines to impress advertisers with the market they offer.

Though new to the field, the Digest, using the services of one of the larger survey-research organizations, devised yet another measurement for gauging the potential of advertising in its pages. It argues that not only numbers of people—and the average United States edition of The Reader's Digest is read by an estimated 32,015,000—but the number of times an issue is picked up for reading is important to the advertiser. Each exposure increases the number of impressions an editorial or an advertising message can make on a customer or prospect. The Reader's Digest, research investigation proved, is picked up and read on the average 5.3 days during the life of an issue, giving it a minimum of 168,210,000 readings.

The vast circulation of The Reader's Digest entails still other considerations and brings it into prominence on other fronts. For every class of mail, first to fourth, The Reader's Digest, before 1958 postal increases, was paying more than $7,000,000 a year, more money than it expends for paper, printing, or any other product the Digest buys. It shares with the country's other magazines and its newspapers the preferential second-class mailing privileges accorded them by Congress in 1879. Congress originally granted, and has since maintained, these privileges—though second-class rates advanced more than 30 per cent between the close of World War II and 1958—to the periodicals of the country because of their informational and educational character. National magazines are considered to function in the national interest because of the continuing education they provide the people of the country and because they are one of the nation's most effective forms of public communication.

The United States Post Office, a political monopoly in perennial financial difficulties, has been subjected to severe criticism in recent years for performing far less efficiently and economically than the postal services of most other important countries of the world. In defense of its own position, though both its system of bookkeeping and its methods of handling mail are known and generally acknowledged to be outmoded and antique, the Post Office has long blamed second-class mail for many of its troubles. The dispute has been going on for at least a half century. In 1910 Edward Bok was using full pages of his *Ladies' Home Journal* to refute Post Office charges.

A. L. Cole acted as spokesman for The Reader's Digest, and, because of the Digest's large postal expenditures, to an extent for the industry, in the widely publicized discussions in the early months of 1958 which saw the Post Office and the periodicals ranged as antagonists.

The magazine position is that Congress, not the Post Office, decides whether periodicals, as a form of continuing public education, should have preferential mailing treatment. It is the public which benefits, just as it benefits from all other forms of tax-supported education. As a matter of national concern the subject falls into Congressional, not Post Office, jurisdiction. The magazines also contend that qualified management, more efficient use of its man power, and the installation and use of even the simplest materials handling equipment in common use throughout private industry would quickly enable the Post Office to wipe out its recurring and loudly announced deficits. As a high official of the department himself described it, the United States Post Office is "one of the most antiquated, antediluvian, obsolete operations in the world."

The magazines as a whole believe the situation would be improved if the Post Office were not quite so antiquated, antediluvian, and obsolete, and if a bookkeeping system comparable to those used in private industry were used to discover and present a more accurate picture of actual Post Office expenses.

The magazines in general and, with some reason, The Reader's Digest in particular believe that American periodicals have an educational purpose and an educational result and that as a powerful force in mass communications they perform a public service of considerable value to the United States.

Under a new postal bill signed into law in May 1958 second-class mailing rates will advance by annual steps over a three-year period another 30 per cent for editorial matter and 60 per cent for advertising.

CHAPTER XXVII

DEWITT WALLACE

The Reader's Digest is what it is because DeWitt Wallace and Lila Acheson Wallace are what they are. It is what they made it consciously and what unconsciously they have expressed through their editing. Pendleton Dudley saw the Wallaces as modest but determined when they first came to live and work over his Pleasantville garage. "They are," he said recently, "just the same now." Then he changed his mind. "The same, but deepened and enriched by years of experience."

Though they are frequently abroad for long periods, the Wallaces live now at High Winds, a three-story house of native stone set high atop a steep hillside on a hundred acres above Byram Lake in Mt. Kisco. The sight commands a wide view of woods and water to the east and a distant overview of the Hudson Valley and the hills beyond it to the west. High Winds was built, as Mrs. Wallace planned in her original sketches, to hug the hilltop on which it stands, the lines of the house following the contours of the land. Stone from old stone walls already on the land was used in the construction of the walls. The pegged studding came from the timbers of ancient barns in the locality. The artisans who worked on the building of the house were encouraged to take their time with the masonry and the fine wood carving of the interior. Often when the Wallaces visited the hilltop on a Sunday to see how the house progressed they had difficulty getting in, as the craftsmen had brought their families on picnics to enjoy the scene and display their handiwork.

Mrs. Wallace, who had been collecting antique furnishings, rugs, crystal, and silver for the house for five years, selected five shades of blue for the Normandy tile roof of High Winds. In the building and decoration she strove throughout for harmony and gentleness, accomplishing the effects she wished through a blending of delicate colors and textures. The Wallaces moved into High Winds in 1937. The first party they gave was for the workmen who had built it.

The Wallaces live unpretentiously at High Winds, entertaining close friends, often Digest editors and business guests, only occasionally a celebrity. They have consistently avoided publicity, neither of them attempting to assume public position commensurate with their accomplishments in the world of mass communications.

Perhaps because of its round, sharply peaked tower, neighbors sometimes refer to High Winds as The Castle. Often Wallace works alone late at night in the tower room, sometimes racing his watch to see how much work he can dispose of in a set time. Where decisions must be reached in borderline cases, whether a manuscript or an important Digest appointment or assignment is in question, he discusses the matter with Mrs. Wallace, and the decision is made jointly. Wallace's capacity for work is as phenomenal as his editorial judgment for the Digest seems unerring. Because of this many of his associates regard him with an unfeigned awe which, definitely, DeWitt Wallace does not share. They speak of his "infallible instinct" for editorial material and can, needlessly, list cases enough in point to give weight to their contention. Wallace is an editor whose achievement can be checked in any estimation of his stature and a publisher whose business acumen can likewise be checked by the record. These same awed associates are often disconcerted by the seeming suddenness and almost casual way in which Wallace reaches and announces decisions of importance.

There are contradictory elements in DeWitt Wallace, as there are contradictory elements in The Reader's Digest. The kindness, clarity, risqué humor, inspirational quality, conservatism—the optimism, masculine directness, the sympathy with the little man, the insistence on clear expression of concrete facts, and sometimes the anger are in the magazine because they are in the man. DeWitt Wallace is often described as elusive and shy. That shyness, almost a diffidence, is apparent with strangers and in his infrequent public appearance. Shy? He is about as shy, a writer who has worked with him closely for many years admitted—whether ruefully or admiringly it was impossible to detect—as a bulldozer. For if he is shy, DeWitt Wallace is also direct. From the beginning he has moved, and moved swiftly, in the straight line which is generally conceded to be the shortest distance between a man and where he wants to go.

Despite the Digest's warnings, DeWitt Wallace was, until recent years, a habitual cigarette smoker. He drinks socially. He enjoys poker but plays only occasionally. Before World War II he flew his own plane from his own landing field at High Winds. He gave his plane to Canada when Britain was sore-pressed in World War II. His fondness for a practical joke and an amusing story are as well known among his associates as his capacity for concentrated effort and swift, clean decision. Tall, lean, of gracious manner, he has a tailored elegance which is not matched by the nondescript old car he drives the seven miles between High Winds and his office in Chappaqua. The Wallaces have been known to wait patiently until one of their European editors, who did not realize who they were, found time to see them. On one trip to Japan, as they were being driven over rough roads through back country, DeWitt Wallace inquired whether the Digest sold many copies in a town they reached. The Digest's Tokyo publisher proudly drove past a bookseller's where a stack of Japanese Digests were on display.

"That pile shows they're *not* selling!" DeWitt Wallace argued jestingly. "Here, I'll sell them." He leaped from the car and began a sales harangue in English while the astonished villagers gathered to watch the antics of the mad foreigner.

A long-time Digest editor seriously explained that he and DeWitt Wallace got along so well because they are both moody and pessimistic. Obviously the close business relationship between Wallace and A. L. Cole is based on the fact that both are clear-minded, practical, and quick to seize on the essentials of a problem. Wallace is confident in those situations involving editorial and business judgment, realms in which aptitudes and developed skills enable him to act with that swift coalescence of recognition, insight, feeling, and judgment which is intuition or, when it is unusually successful, inspiration. It is likely that what DeWitt Wallace sees he sees immediately, and that which he does not see immediately he does not see at all or further concern himself with.

Once when the family was about to return from Wooster to

St. Paul, DeWitt Wallace hid atop the luggage piled on the wagon ready to take them all to the railroad station. Some of the luggage slipped and he tumbled, clattering to the road in the midst of the family prayers he had been trying to avoid. The six-year-old boy made the journey back to Minnesota in disgrace and with a lump on his head. It was not the only time DeWitt Wallace reacted against the restrictions enforced by his strict Presbyterian upbringing, but youthful rebellion is seldom a total defense against being influenced by the tenets and practices of an established spiritual discipline. DeWitt Wallace was imbued with the values and ideals preached and practiced in his Macalester environment. Lila Acheson Wallace too grew up with the ideals and practical energy that combine to form the atmosphere of the ministerial missionary household. Even while it was still an entirely eclectic periodical, The Reader's Digest reflected the inherited traditions imbedded in the characters of its editors.

Wallace allocates large responsibilities to associates whom he trusts, reserving only the power of final decision. At the same time he retains personal control over comparatively minor affairs. Perhaps because he is deeply aware of the importance of its personnel to the production of the Digest, he personally approves or disapproves appointments to even minor editorial and executive posts and checks carefully on the performance of men during the probationary period of their employment. Despite his swiftly made and almost casually announced decisions where major policies and sometimes very large sums of money are involved, Wallace will sometimes defer consideration of a lesser problem until it is defunct through neglect. Sometimes, possibly to temper sustained intensity of purpose and effort with the relief that makes it supportable, possibly for his own amusement, he will approach a minor matter by some circuitous route which baffles more prosaic travelers.

DeWitt Wallace has been known to lose his way while showing important visitors about the Digest headquarters, then have to ask directions back to his own office. His courteous, almost gentle, manner is sometimes mildly abstracted, but even at such times there is no mistaking the alertness, the vitality repressed just beneath the surface. The editorial wisdom, the business acumen, the astuteness stay; and there is another constant. Always Wallace is eager to credit Lila Acheson Wallace with more than he can quite express. He makes it clear that no important Digest post has ever been filled without her knowledge and approval, says that her intuitive understanding of people tells her more about a person in five minutes than anyone else could find out in five years. He even says that, by creating the atmosphere in which he could work best at what is of central and consuming importance to them both, "I think Lila made the Digest possible." In his later sixties, gray-haired DeWitt Wallace has the thoughtful but unlined and youthful face of a man who for a long time has been doing, and doing well and successfully, what in life he most wants to do.

Wallace can be blandly elusive. Sometimes he is in Florida when important members of his staff believe he is at High Winds. He may call a writer or an editor from Arizona when he is thought to be in Europe. Actually one of the ranking staff members at Chappaqua always knows where Wallace is, but it is not always the same man, and others may have no idea at all of Wallace's whereabouts.

Wherever he is, The Reader's Digest is uppermost in Wallace's mind. His habit is to write and address his own Christmas cards. Almost always the personal message carries some reference to the Digest. When the fancy seizes him Wallace sends other cards. On a recent trip it occurred to him to send an oversized card to the secretary of one of his top editors. On it, very legibly, he asked whether reports were true that during his absence the editor had become a confirmed alcoholic. If this were so, didn't she have any influence over him? It might help if she became an alcoholic herself, then joined Alcoholics Anonymous and reformed. This, Wallace added, was "just a casual suggestion." In an indignant reply the secretary heatedly denied every charge against the maligned editor, whom she described as a model of probity and sobriety. Wallace was delighted.

This occasional impishness can be disconcerting. More than one of his staff has more than once replied seriously when the intent of a Wallace memorandum was facetious; or, to his greater embarrassment, responded flippantly to a serious suggestion.

If he likes a piece DeWitt Wallace will print it. If he does not like it he will not print it, no matter who wrote it. The central fact about The Reader's Digest is as simple as that. Wallace will seldom attempt to explain his acceptance or rejection. If pressed, he is apt to quote an *obiter dictum* of Lord Mansfield, eighteenth-century Lord Chief Justice of England: "Give your decisions, never your reasons; your decisions may be right. Your reasons are sure to be wrong."

Actually, what DeWitt Wallace is and is not is down for everyone to read. Inevitably the full extent of his powers and the complexities of his character are revealed in detail in the volumes of The Reader's Digest published since February 1922. The relationship of a man and his creation is such that The Reader's Digest is more DeWitt Wallace than is DeWitt Wallace himself.

CHAPTER XXVIII

CONCLUSION

"The Best Investment I Ever Made," A. J. Cronin reported, was when, as a young doctor in crowded London, he saved the life of a young boy who had attempted suicide in remorse for stealing seven pounds, ten shillings to gamble with. Cronin put up the money. An understanding police sergeant decided to make no report. The rooming-house landlady offered a month's free board. Years later the novelist met the man aboard ship. He was a successful and useful social worker. Cronin told the story in The Reader's Digest.

The world-famous musician and medical missionary, Albert Schweitzer, told Fulton Oursler why he felt that helping others was a man's second job in life. It was a Digest story in 1949. Inspiration and hope, faith and courage, are an essential part of the Digest story. So is the heroic epic, whether it be "Lou Gehrig's Epic of Courage" or the thrilling adventure of *Kon-Tiki* or the World War II story of "Chaplains Courageous."

Medical miracles, marriage, moving biographies, outspoken attacks on the maladministration of public affairs or the mishandling of social problems; consumer reports on everything from vitamin preparations and mouthwashes to watch repairing; art-of-living advice, the art of love to the art of buying a secondhand car—these too are characteristic Digest subjects.

The sentimental and tender story, the tense revelation, the sharply critical exposé are always there: *Journey for Margaret,* "The Enemy's Masterpiece of Espionage" by J. Edgar Hoover, "Ridiculous Waste in the Armed Services." The drive to religious belief is there, whether in an article describing the indomitable faith of an immigrant family enduring bitter hardships, in precepts like "Seven Reasons Why a Scientist Believes in God," or in a heart-warming parable from Steinbeck's *The Grapes of Wrath.* There is related material in articles that either dance the titillated reader on the edge of tingling mysteries or cut deep into the quick of life—"The Wonders of Conception," "Sexual License: Key to Soviet Strategy," "Artificial Insemination—Has It Made Happy Homes?"

In between and around and through pieces as different as "The Facts About a Guaranteed Annual Wage," "Lift Up Your Eyes to Marvel," and "Red China, the World's Biggest Dope Peddler" are the stories of the unusual in the commonplace, the human, the humorous, the lovable, and the ridiculous. All through are the minds and imaginations of the writers, scientists, actors, politicians, poets, doctors, businessmen, missionaries, soldiers, peasants, talking or talked about in Digest stories.

Such are the ingredients. The Digest is varied and alive. The mix is rich and warm. Yet, like the complete individual, a good magazine is considerably more than the sum of its many parts. Like the individual, it is the cumulative result of its own experience and lives as if it had always been and always will be. It arouses emotions and provokes attitudes that often have little to do with what is contained in a particular issue. For many millions The Reader's Digest is both a living entity of recognizable dimensions and characteristics and a continuous translation of life into understandable human terms.

To its readers the Digest is simple, sincere, and warmly human. The Digest operates to reduce baffling complexities to understandable simplicities. It puts abstract problems into human terms and world concerns into personal frame. The Digest makes at least some of life's confusion seem intelligible. It entertains as it instructs, amuses as it describes the contemporary scene, and seems to convey not only its own warmth and friendliness but also the warmth and friendliness of other people to the reader. Informed by vitality and compassion, an animal heat in its stories of wild life, an earthiness in its stories of the domesticated human animal, but an affirmation and an optimism running through them all, it offers hope always and says always that hope is a good thing.

Because of its humanness, because it both stimulates and reassures, The Reader's Digest provokes an emotional as well as an intellectual response, more of an emotional than a cerebral response. It arouses gratitude as it awakens interest. People respond to the Digest as need responds to affection. They respond with affection and trust. The Digest is clear at a time when clarity is increasingly hard to come by. The Digest is emotional. The Digest is sentimental. The Digest is itself trusting and indignant when trust is exploited or violated.

There is enough in life to divert. There is more than enough cleverness for all the dazzling brilliance and intellectual gymnastics, all the exhibitionism and brittle self-confidence the most worldly can wish. Men and women tire of it. Sometimes, though fascinated, they feel inadequate and lose confidence that they can successfully imitate or even cope with it all. The Digest offers the reader a simpler and homelier relationship to the world, and he is grateful. This may be why the Digest has its strong appeal for the successful, well educated, and highly placed as well as for the less successful, less well educated who are placed nowhere at all. As generally understood but sometimes forgotten, Judy O'Grady, the colonel's lady, and a whole host of politicians, corporation heads, housewives, professors, and mechanics are still sisters under the skin. Most people respond to warmth and kindness, and The Reader's Digest, whatever else it is or is not, is warm, kinder, and less pretentious than many of the people readers, perforce, must live with.

I like my dog, and he likes me. I used to like the dog I had when I was small and I was home. I like this dog in the Digest too—or this great man, who is like the old man who used to live down the street, and this woman who reminds me of that friend of Mother's. It is a little like that.

The Reader's Digest is not things which it does not pretend to be. It does not go into exhaustive detail on any subject. It is not often analytical. It is not bitter or cynical or superior, or up-to-the-minute with its news and interpretations of the news, or even splendidly pictorial. It is DeWitt Wallace with all the strength, the hopes, anxieties, and inconsistencies of the complicated individual. Millions of readers, consciously or unconsciously, recognize these as characteristics they know and share. They are sometimes afraid and want to be brave. They are depressed and want to be cheered. They worry about sex, fear it, exult in it. They hope. They relish the humor in life when they can find it. They hate unfairness and resent the abuse of the weak by the strong. They like miracles and thrill to high adventure. They have a grave regard for facts. They approve substantiation of the beliefs they share with their myriad fellows.

The Reader's Digest does not reach its world audience of perhaps 70,000,000 readers by being profound, esoteric, and difficult to understand—or by espousing unpopular causes or adopting viewpoints either outmoded or too far advanced. It reaches it through wide coverage, balance and variety, and the personal applicability of the material it prints. It reaches it partly through the compression that means that only the high spots of a discussion can be presented, and these set forth in black and white clarity. It reaches it partly because Digest opinions are usually unqualified. The reader is left in no doubt where the magazine stands on an issue. What it dislikes it hates; what it approves it loves. So does the reader. The Digest reaches its world audience mostly because DeWitt Wallace is able to translate his own feelings and attitudes, his sense of man's kinship, his curiosity, interests, beliefs, and convictions, into instructive, entertaining, and inspiring terms. The Reader's Digest does it month after month, year after year, in a continuing relationship that long ago seems to have transcended the artificialities of print and paper.

Despite all this, The Reader's Digest did not grow unaided. As they must be for the popular acceptance of any idea, the times were propitious. The Digest began shortly after World War I when hurry began and what has been called "the decline of attention" set in. The short, easily read condensed article was matched to the hurry. The Digest rose with the spread and spreading thin of education. More people could read, and they were hungry for facts; fewer people could manage abstruse reading matter. During the economic depression of the 1930s, when the

Digest reached full stature, it offered hope and inspiration to people who badly needed them and the best from all the other magazines at a price which was all that most people could afford. During World War II servicemen yearned for news of home and the civilian public was hungry for information and entertainment. The circulations of all the popular magazines grew, that of the Digest far more than most. After the war the Digest drove for world circulation just as people became, and perforce remained, sharply aware of the rest of the world, and Americans became internationalists of necessity. None of these facts made or could make The Reader's Digest the phenomenon among magazines that it is, but circumstances nicely concurred, and the Digest used them shrewdly. It could, for the appeal and the power were in it from the first.

At its best the Digest has an almost Wordsworthian quality. It can light the commonplace. At its worst it is diluted Barrie. More often it keeps a Dickensian mean. It has blood in it and a darting curiosity. It is for everybody. It takes a bright look around at all it can see and reports brightly on all it has seen. It relishes a joke, thrills to the story of high adventure, but delights to find the extraordinary in the ordinary. It prefers the positive, likes the sunlighted picture best. It is directed to the same characteristics in the reader that it displays itself, the curiosity, the humor, the love of adventure, the affection for the familiar, the desire to understand, the indignation at what hurts, the wish that things were better, and the belief that they can be.

Perhaps the most valuable possession of The Reader's Digest is the essential loneliness of the human heart.